Coming of The Light

The Dawn of Spiritual Inspiration

D.M. Ferrari

Biography

David Ferrari is a licensed general contractor, freelance copywriter and an author. He lives in Florida with his wife Kathy and their chocolate lab, Muddo. As a universal spiritualist, David has an affinity for the messages of Jesus, Lao Tsu and Emerson. His twenty year journey of love, compassion, self discovery and the complete scope of life's triumphs and travails is related in this raw, real, spiritual poetry-driven tale of an ordinary guy who was blessed enough to be shown a life of conscious union with our source. A life literally saved with the written word.

Table of Contents

Dedication

First, as the bestower of blessings and the foremost recipient of my gratitude, I thank and dedicate this book to God. No matter what dogma you currently labor under, or whatever your concept of God is; even if you have no concept at all. In the following pages I hope to *let* enough of "the imprisoned splendor" escape so that Her light may help you become aware of the infinite wonders of a serene inner life. I do not know who God *is,* I do not know what God *is,* I do not know if God *is* divine. Supreme, yes. But to me, divine, even though I use it in my writing, elicits thoughts of the pious, unreachable God, separate and apart from his beloved offspring. If organized building bound religion is how you pray, more peace to you. I sit at the beach at sunrise (nature is my church) and as I watch His day become, I am certain of only one thing: God *IS.*

IS offers no explanations of profound discovery. No grandiose statements of the herd accepted facts of God's depth and demeanor. No rigid tenets about how one is to live their life. No dogma dictating how one is to worship. No reward of heaven in the luxurious clouds, and no punishment of hell in the fiery bowels. Just *IS. IS* merely says yes to life. *IS* acknowledges the fact that the intricacies of our world, our universe and especially we humans could not be cosmic happenstance. *IS* acknowledges the glaring fact that evolution still required creation and by its very nature can be considered nothing other than intelligent design. *IS* understands that humans as they exist today are not the apex of evolution but awaits the day when we **consciously** realize that we are spirit having a human experience, rather than the other way around.

Here comes your day
Filled with thy grace
I write and I pray
Please, show me thy face.

So many of my rhymes
concern the rising sun
The most glorious times
Spent with The One

Man could not paint
A picture so precise
The brush would surely taint
Never could it suffice

I sit here in awe
My receptive mind a blank
A frozen heart to thaw
Just One to thank.

The clouds are perfection
The colors are aflame
Yet, just a reflection
Of the invisible name.

Expansion of the soul
Ego does contract
Here ego has no role
And that is a fact.

Mind can not comprehend
The creators perfection unfolding
With love She does tend

With love I am beholding.

The reds and the blues
The orange and the white
The birth of spectacular hues
What a mesmerizing sight.

To not mention the purple
Would be a crime
Nothing rhymes with purple
Still, that's just fine.

The sun's first peak
So succulent, so warm
I have nothing to seek
Nothing but the norm.

The rays pierce my eyes
Yet, I can not look away
Human logic it defies
That's all I need say.

ॐ

The golden orb rises majestically from a languid sea
My soul is at peace viewing such perfection
The gull hovers, encased in a succulent ocean breeze
Connecting me like a silken thread to what *is.*

There is no thought of flight, just being
There is no awareness of air, just existence
The fish swimming below knows not of water
There is no perception of being wet.

The coconut palm dances to loves song
Gazing upon them I 'see' they are barren of fruit
Yet, can I trust in a conception born of sight
Their fruit omnipresent awaits its season.

The sand beneath my feet is just sand
Or is that a judgement made with opaque vision
For what *is,* can never be "just"
It's essence, the stuff of life, as I.

The sand fleas that bite me are truly a nuisance
Surely such an annoying creature is not necessary
What do i know of necessary
Life manifests for a purpose i could never
comprehend.

I do not need to know why
Contrary to the human need for intellectual
understanding
Knowing i will never know is a pleasing reliance
Believing that i understand, i truly Do Not!

I sit alone in the stillness of infinity
Listening to the breeze, I am aware of sublime
companionship
Mind relegated unto least, I am most
In the nothingness of pure being, I am everything.

One with the beach grass, the beach plum, the
hopeful fisherman
It was Emerson who said, "one with God is a majority"
In such an awareness love pervades
Where there is love, there is knowing, I know "what"
you are.

Eyes closed, I await the announcement of Her will
Yesterday forgotten, tomorrow exists not, lead me
Now
There is no hunger dwelling at the feast of the Divine
Sanctify me, use me to bestow thy grace to others.

When traversing darkness, the wise obtain
illumination
Yet, most seek such safety in the external realm
How is one to find, possessing knowledge not of
where to look
True illumination teaches, we are all The Light sought.

I ask, how does a carpenter become a writer?
In the same way as a carpenter became "The Way"
How does an obtuse mind learn of spirit?
With absolute certainty i say, "i do not know"

Why do I follow a path with directions unknown
You don't need directions when you have a guide
Why do I trust a guide I've only recently met
Because He is the path, and also the destination.

ॐ

The relentless howling wind drives stinging rain and
spray into my face at 6 a.m.
To me it feels like the hand of rapture washing some
grime from my being
A clearer transparency for thee.

As gentle as a lover, the ocean does embrace
Tenderly it occupies my most sacred space
Entranced, as if it knows my very soul
On my lips, I taste her salty spray
I need not a building, this is where I pray
In this reverence, I am most whole.

My skin tingles in mornings cool breeze
Of all your offerings, this one please
Each blessed breath sweet and exotic
My face bathed by the warming sun
The transition to light, is the time of The One
The waves crash, soothing and melodic.

Thank you God, thank you for this
Even just a moment, is eternal bliss
Your creation has awed me in many a place
The mountains, the meadows, a majestic forest of
trees
I also have deep love for all of these
Yet, my heart always returns to this space.

ॐ

Second, all my love and gratitude to my family. Nikki, who was born at the outset of my spiritual journey, so, in essence we were children learning from and teaching each other. Anthony, whose gentle and jovial manner keeps me grounded. Every poet needs one, and Kathy has been my muse for 38 years (highschool sweethearts); thanks babe.

Ladies, this is primarily a book celebrating love and life through spiritual poetry, so I felt it important to tell you that even if he is incapable of voicing it, this is how your guy feels about the love of his life.

Mere words the point they would miss,
Of to me what she means
In those green windows I find my bliss
Her being the stuff of dreams.

ॐ

When I wrote that it felt like so much more wanted to come out, and I probably could have gone on for pages. Yet, in reading the first stanza I knew that no matter how long a poem I wrote, I could not say it any better. Gentlemen, if your wife hasn't read that poem and you need to use it for dog house egress, please be my guest. Do not forget to use the correct eye color though.

A union of divine proportions
Free from harmful distortions
Merged souls dwell not in fate
Two hearts on display,
As we giggle and play
God, I love our Kate.

Pink and blue braces,
The most adorable faces
A dance move with a twirl
See how she grows,
Her cup overflows
God, I love our girl.

Running and jumping,
I always get a good thumping
We battle with hysterical joy
The face of my son,
We are not two but one

God, I love our boy.
Eyes that were shut,
Had no chance to rebut
Spirit they just could not see
Then the gaze turned inside,
Suddenly open wide
Thank you, I love me.

The flowers, trees and grass,
A sweetly shaped… apple
The luminescence of a pearl
The cardinals joyous tune,
The ocean shimmers under the moon
God, I love your world.

My being does expand,
Subject to loves' command
It flows through me in verse
The planets hurtle through space,
A synchronized cosmic race
God, I love your universe.

The grace and the glory
Revealer of my story
Within me struck rapturous chord
So I dwell in the space,
Where I can see Her face
God I love my Lord.

ॐ

Introduction

I guess at this point it would be prudent to explain that in my writing if I use a lowercase i, it is not a typo; I am referring to the limited human sense of being. I endeavor to use the correct punctuation and syntax in my commentary. However, I write it like I hear it, so my poetry won't always follow the rules. Poetry in italics are spontaneous emanations that occur when thoughts formulate, bubble up, and seek release. When referring to God in my writing I use He, She, Him, Her, Mother, Father, Source, Essence, It and I interchangeably. When speaking of God, most of us say he and have a picture of a wizened old man with a flowing white beard up on a cloud in the heavens. God *is* Spirit/Consciousness, and that has no gender, or description for that matter.

My teacher **Joel S. Goldsmith**, the founder of *The Infinite Way*, termed God 'The Infinite Invisible,' which is as accurate a description as one could possibly offer.

The thought of infinity is something that we can not wrap our human minds around. All the grains of sand on all the beaches in all the world are countable, an absurd notion to count even a handful, but not infinite. All the stars in the night sky, also countable... not infinite, or are they? It's an expanding universe.

I hear, taste, smell,
I touch and I see
But, it is the sense of the soul that grasps infinity.

ॐ

Invisible is something that we can not see. If we can not see it, how could it be possible for us to know it well enough to attach a description? It is not possible to know or fathom the depth and breadth of God by means of human intelligence. **Lao-tzu,** the enlightened Chinese philosopher profoundly stated in the *Tao Te Ching* that, "The Tao that can be described is not the eternal Tao. The name that can be spoken is not the eternal name." In other words, If you can describe it… that ain't it!!

God is an experience within the serene sanctuary of self, available in the silence, when we have stilled our mind of all the unrelenting inane chatter that is so detrimental to our positive state of being.

We view a person plodding down the street
Arguing with themself, obviously insane
With the symptoms of crazy, they are replete
We judge, because from such, we refrain?

ॐ

You and I happen to be blessed with possession of the filters that keep us from appearing crazy. Yet, we all walk around all day with those self defeating, soul sucking, crazy thoughts and private confrontations, that continuously flow across the perpetual movie reel in our mind, which we could accurately term, "the crazy files."

I write from a christian point of reference, yet I consider myself a universal spiritualist. There is light inherent in any true path or person. If you have light to share, by all means let it shine and please accept my gratitude. When I write of Christ, it is not the man I speak of. The man was Jesus, and he was The Christ. The Christ *is* the manifestation of the Spirit of God in man. Obviously, if one speaks of The Christ you think Jesus, but we also have Buddha, Mohammed, Shankaracharya and many others who attained conscious oneness with our Source. This oneness *is* the very essence of what I am, what you are, what we all are.

Still, I am not talking religion. If I speak of religion, we can then take sides and retreat into our conditioned reactions and responses to something so flammable as "my" path, "my" prophet, "my" God. Yet, no matter the name of your prophet or god, you are reading this, so you are conscious, or infinite consciousness manifesting as individual consciousness to be specific. You are the spark! you are the essence!

Verily, the reason I write from a christian standpoint is because Jesus in His Enlightened eloquence summed up my spirituality in the first two all encompassing words of, in my opinion, the most profound prayer ever voiced. ***Our Father.***

I am not a buddhist
And, yet I am
I am a disciple of The Christ
Who sees the beauty in Islam.

My individual being is paramount
Yet, likened to a grain of sand
In voice I mount up to heaven
Yet, I'm still just part of the band.

I am the way I am
Because you are the way you are
Perception says we are earthbound

Still, my heart sees you in a star.

I tread with care on mother earth
Sweet reverence of all I am seeing
How can we live any other way?
For all of creation is interbeing.

I dare not dwell in malice or disrespect
Gazing upon you, I see me
I dare not chain a brother in bondage
For then, it is I that is not free.

This grand existence is an intricate mesh
All of creation is inter-related
I shall not affix a preconceived label
With a closed mind, beauty negated.

With a knowing heart, I seek truth
It resides not in intolerance and gloom
The flower sowed under a shroud
Shall never have the light to bloom.

Seeds of love and compassion I water daily
Through me, I pray, His will be done
A soul in peace shall always see
One in all, all in The One.

ॐ

Now, Jesus was a practicing rabbi who was traveling with, while teaching and preaching to those of the Jewish faith. Yet, he did not say, "Yahweh our Hebrew God." He just said, "Our Father." Much of Jesus' teachings were cloaked in allegory and parables, and therefore subject to much interpretation over two thousand years. But these two words are as clear and concise as possible, and by their all inclusiveness leave no room for interpretation other than: There is One God who is parent to all of us, and whether we know it or not, like it or not, that makes all of us brothers and sisters.

Chapter One: Baby Steps

At the time when my spiritual journey began i had been suffering from chronic, crippling back pain for about 15 years. In 1985 or so, being young, dumb and supremely overconfident in my indestructible physicality as most young men are, I stopped a piece of scaffolding equipment from crushing my customers brand new Cadillac. Smooth move asshole, it bent you over backwards and crushed you instead. One bad decision on a construction site and my life changed forever. Now, hearing that you would say it changed for the worse, and after too many years of agony i would not have disagreed.

However, if i did not live with so much pain I would never have started searching for a way to heal myself. An honest doctor told me point blank, "We don't have the technology to fix you, deal with it as long as you can and by then, maybe?" Without that kick in the teeth I would have never committed to a life of mind and body in service to spirit and stumbled upon my path to salvation, meditation, and meditation combined with kundalini yoga, as put forth in another of those life changing books *Meditation as Medicine,* by Dr. Dharma Singh Khalsa.

Dr. Dharma is an M.D. and a yogi, and as such has a very unique perspective on the mind, body, spirit connection as it pertains to healing and unifying all three vital elements. While in the serene sanctuary of meditation, I learned to be receptive and keep an open listening ear for impartations from within. The first time I achieved a deep meditation I was absolutely stunned by the serenity of the silence.

It's not like I actually heard the words but I had a dialogue meandering across the screen of consciousness and i was not the thinker. I know, I know, but my meditator's will back me up on this. Please, tell 'em i'm not nuts.

What I receive in silence,
Truth revealed
It is my purest reliance,
Naught concealed.

How is it that I hear,
The word
Clearly as if by ear,
Yet unheard.

To the mind it makes no sense,
Saving grace
If it did, just pretense,
Crowded space.

Gratitude is in my heart,
Compassion felt
Love flows off the chart,
Avarice melt.

I have let go of rage,
Open soul
So sweet to turn that page,
Feeling whole.

so very few see our Source,
Ignorant eyes
They follow not my course,
A surprise?

I would love to share,
No receptivity

My soul would I bare,
No proclivity.

This secret I do keep,
locked away
Infinite wisdom to reap,
… Some day.

Grace is available now,
Her will
There is only one way how,
Be still.

The flow is ending here,
Bowing head
I Am ever near,
God said.

ॐ

What I was hearing and seeing, no wait, it was neither of those things. It was what I was experiencing. It felt like an intimate interaction with the seer of what's seen (*I Am I, in back of these eyes*), the knower of what's known, the speaker of the spoken and it said:

"Here my child follow this path, write my words, although you know not whence they come, or what they truly mean, yet. Thou my child with no literary skills whatsoever, let me guide you. Learn of me, for I Am the source of all the verse ever written. Be of the spirit which is gentle and joyful. Your anger, your rage, your outbursts will not do! Here my son is your path,

your outlet, your road to within, which is the only place
you can commune with me."

It was truly astounding when this knowing did begin
I couldn't explain, I just knew that i knew
Not a game of chance, nothing to win
The less i became, the more I grew.

I had my eyes closed, how was it I was seeing?
With a million words I could never explain
I am one with, yet can't fathom, Infinite being
Long held perceptions became rather inane.

The human joy I felt in an instant turned to rage
Buffeted about violently in human duality
The door never locked, still i remained in minds cage
Lamenting the decline in my ailing mortality.

My son, you've but to knock
The door will open without a squeak
You are individual consciousness, yet just part of the
flock
The journey within is how you must seek.

When God says "jump," you only ask, how high?
When She says be still, you rest back in Her peace
When His truth He reveals, you ask not why
When She says judge not, you cease.

With just a grain of knowing comes profound gratitude
For the light in darkness, that seems puny and small
Please teach me, please lead me, my souls attitude
Possessing no "things," then I can truly give all.

ॐ

i had been bumbling around with some rhyming thoughts prior to this, but it was the drivel of someone with less than no clue. i was trying to express profound truths for which i had no basis, or skills, yet. After meditating for a while i was becoming more centered and less reactionary, and my writing was showing signs of improvement. Seriously, it had nowhere else to go but up. This next one came out after a particularly serene meditation and it is truly the first spiritual poem I ever wrote. It is titled "Hand of God."

Everywhere I look, I see the hand of God
Years and years i stumbled
an unseeing clod.

Awareness, love and compassion
Brings the vision of an eagle
Life's spiritual peasant
Now knows the loft of regal.

The beauty of a flower
The song the lark does sing
He is everywhere and nowhere
Infusing every living thing.

Yet, life is no prerequisite
For a jaw to drop
Gaze upon the splendor
Of a sun-lit mountain top.

The sea is where he started
Yet, water is not alive
Spectacular creatures abound
Where I could not survive.

A speck of life, a creature so immense
It weighs ten thousand pounds
The universal vibration
Infinitely silent
Yet, we hear the sounds.

As I'm writing
I revel
In a birds
song of joy
I watched with indescribable awe
At the birth of our boy.

Without God i suffered
Unspeakable physical pain
He allowed me the time
To find my way home
His love always did remain.

My spirit and my body
Innate intelligence to heal
Alone
surely to crumble
No possibility to feel.

With all hope gone
My spirit dashed
A pill my only friend
He spoke unto me of only guidance
My Soul
I would have to tend.

The guidance he chose
As my salvation
Came in the form of the written word
My path began to straighten

My vision no longer blurred.

Clearly I now see my spiritual journey
Is about compassion,
Trust and love
I give myself over completely
To the only way
To rise above.

I had to travel
To the depths of despair
As if i was alone
Then the light
Was revealed to me
My path, clearly shown.

It spoke directly to my soul
"My son
do you finally understand?"
Yes I do
Now and forever
I will hold Your loving hand.

ॐ

Even though this is not the best I've written, it is probably my favorite. In this poem I see the birth of the seeker; searching for something that he has less than no clue where to find. You may have noticed me say that a pill was my only friend. At this point, my life was a twisted dichotomy of searing physical agony inter dispersed with meditation that provided me with a brief respite of joyous release as often as I could find a quiet space. I began journaling in 1996 when my daughter was born. Once I opened the gates, it didn't take long for spiritual poetry to start flooding out in a torrent and flow across the screen of consciousness that I was endeavoring to become one with. It came when I was driving, in a meeting, on a roof and it would wake me from a sound sleep. I am not what you would call a technology guy. However, my information was coming from the only source of technology that never becomes obsolete. Is it a coincidence that we were approaching the new Millennium and the age of Aquarius?

My intention had been to leave my children a legacy of information. We all know the family stories of love and loss, triumph and failure; but how many of us know our parents, truly. My children would. I even showed them that frightening place, you know, that place where we strip off the mask that we present to the world, even our family.

Now, God help me… literally, I'm showing it to you. To be perfectly honest this is some scary shit! Sorry, I curse now and then. Which I will warn you of by placing an * at the top of a poem. I will curse no more in the commentary, as cursing is just me making an extreme point to myself in my poetry. Bearing your soul to itself and your children is daunting and revelatory enough, but in revealing myself to you, scary stuff just didn't fly. One thing I will not do is debate my spirituality. I write what is given to me. If you disagree or have an issue with something I wrote, free will entitles you to your opinion and to read what is more in tune with your light. To say i am apprehensive in taking on this endeavor is a massive understatement, as I have always played my spiritual cards close to the vest.

Sacred and secret the word must remain

From divulging our pearl we must refrain
It's our place of shelter in the driving rain
Such secrecy at times makes me a little insane.

This knowing it seems no one else knows
I sway in harmony as the mighty wind blows
It hurts to see a brother mired in the throes
Their fruit, it withers as mine it grows.

Yet, i myself know I'm nothing
Just a mere servant in the palace of the king
Naked as a newborn, except for this ring
Knowing such joy, why should I not sing.

I do not sing outwardly, the lyrics not complete
With human limitations i am replete
To think any other is treachery and conceit
I have much work to do at the masters feet.

One with our source, the only stature I can claim
I'm learning to judge not, ascribing no blame
Known as David, but that is not my true name
The ravenous beast termed "ego" shall become tame.

With my brothers and sisters, I so want to share
But, i have nothing to give, so i do not dare
Unless it's Spirit speaking, you get a blank stare
So, for now, a God experience is my only care.

In terms of love, that seems rather cold
Still, standing fast to withinness, is truly bold
In the silence, I am clay, for God's mould
With no words to explain, it must remain untold.

Yet, I must share that is spiritually right

With clarity of soul we espouse the light
I must *let* it shine for those with sight
Only with Her wings can I take flight.

The mighty oak tree has nothing to say
Even behind clouds the sun shines every day
A closed mouth, an open soul, I let God pray
I can only get lost if i lead the way.

If I am still enough, then others will find
The spiritual impulse illumines no matter if blind
Words have no authority, produced of mind
As personal sense fades, there is no axe to grind.

There is no struggle, only my peace
This you shall know when desires do cease
Infinitely unfolding truth shall never decrease
Life's friction hinders not with spiritual grease.

With a billion words it will never be explained
The world's majority do serve, their master, ingrained
The universe still expands because it can't be
contained
The earth did melt, Spirit is all that remained.

ॐ

So few know of what I speak
Submission to the invisible a joke
Fewer still know of being meek
So, I am guarded with words thus spoke
I surely gets blurred, nary a word
Infinity contained not in speech
It is fore, aft and flank
Yet, my mind is a blank

My stillness is how I beseech.
What's viewed as indifference is really compassion
A headless chicken I never more will be
To know The Christ is not in fashion
Mortalities slave knows naught of free
I dare not speak of what it is I seek
What *is,* I shall not voice
This knowing no longer mine
If cast before swine
Silence, the only prudent choice.

Even those closest know not my life
The depth or the extent of my zeal
Leaving no visible scars, this razor sharp knife
That daily slices away the unreal.
A sword not peace, does afford release
Non- attachment to every condition
For the good is as untrue
As the evil that i do
Subject to either, the path to perdition.

At the very least to most, I'm awfully strange
My life centered in the unheard, the unseen
Yet, I feel my Soul affecting change
There are two worlds and I'm in between.
What a twist, i must die to exist
For the human mind all to confusing
Of spiritual truth I'm on the brink
Then i stumble, start to think
I'm sure God finds my thick head amusing.

My dear child, you silly, silly boy
You are spinning your wheels round and round
Still, I love you so, my ultimate joy
Flesh not worth a penny for a pound.
The true spiritual measure, where is your treasure

For there also your heart will be
Do you desire money and fame
Or to know my true name?
This truth even a blind man could see.

Let the unknowing think as they will
For The Christ they will always crucify
The cross of ignorance shall not kill
Even in the valley I Am shall supply
In One I rely, though you may ask why
An answer understood, i can not give
Love, life, truth and protection
Meets hate, death, fear and rejection
The world opinion dictates not, I live!

ॐ

At this point in time I started carrying a micro recorder because I just couldn't keep up with what was flowing out. Until I was blessed with the realization that the manna falls fresh every day, every moment.

"There is no need to lay it up for tomorrow. I will provide fresh and new sustenance as it is necessary for your unfoldment. Just remain open to the flow and acknowledge me in all thy ways and I shall direct your path."

As the words flow in procession
Thy omniscience grants me expression
my humanness beats hasty secession
God is, is all I know.

I used to express from rage
Pacing inside minds cruel cage

No use of anything sage
Not aware of divinity's flow.

To my bewilderment and great shock
Thy love removed the lock
You bade me, "come join my flock"
It was not possible to say no.

"Yes father," is all I could say
Thou revealed to me how to pray
My Dwelling Place, forever and a day
It was then that I started to grow.

Mortal ailments miraculously healed
My stature as joint heir, you revealed
In an instant my fate was sealed
A transparency for Spirits glow.

Quite confused was i at first
As my heart's malice was dispersed
My arid Soul no longer did thirst
You chose me, privy to the show.

For my past you did not chide
My child seek not, nor can you hide
For my kingdom is inside
Here and now life's breath does blow.

ॐ

Except for journaling or writing this book I rarely if ever sit down with the intention of writing. Unless of course I'm feeling down and in need of sublime companionship. **Wolfgang Von Goethe** once wrote, "Only engage, and then the mind grows heated; Begin it, and the work will be completed." This has always been how I feel whenever I am led to grab my pen. I engage and that invisible something, which is the greatest part of our being, takes over and illuminates whatever is necessary to my unfoldment at that particular time. If I was talking sports I would say I was in the zone.

I have always felt that the writing comes through me rather than from me, and I am merely the instrument that consciousness uses as Its scribe. As such, 50% of any profit that is generated from my writing will be donated. Whoa, hold on there putz, do you really want to learn the lesson of spiritual pride again? That will be 65% donated, so i always remember that i, David, am the lesser part of this collaboration. As a parent my light says that St. Jude's and Shriners hospitals are easy choices. As an American, even though war is not my thing, people are, so wounded warriors, is also an easy choice.

These first three, and I hesitate to call them charities, (however, I know of no word that means compassion as an action) are well known and most likely universally accepted as noble and worthy of our respect and donations. However, this fourth one, unless you have suffered the harrowing trials and tribulations of a direct association is most likely not on your radar. NEDA, the national eating disorders association came to my attention as most lesser known compassionate actions do, the direct association of loved ones. My two very dear friends had this association with NEDA and ultimately suffered every parents worst nightmare. Yet, that is a family story and in no way mine to tell. So, I will stop here and only say this; If you would experience the story, of a girl, whose name was not merely a lovely sounding parental preference, but became the essence, of the woman. Then please visit Gracehollandcozine.org. Thank you so very much.

Before I ever write a word I meditate/pray and ask that as a beholder, please let me be a clear transparency for the blessing of creative enlightenment. Please do not misunderstand and think I'm holding myself up as enlightened, or some kind of preacher or teacher. I am None of those things!! To say, or even think, i am spiritually enlightened is akin to spiritual suicide. Spiritual pride is an obtuse, ugly, self defeating thing. A lesson i learned a short way into my journey, just when i started to think i knew something. Silly, silly boy!

*

I've read many books, i talk the talk
A little truth do i know
So, why is it, i can't walk the walk
My obtuseness, the star of the show.

It's been years I'm on the path
How is it i still get lost?
For my thick head i incur the wrath
Daily i must pay the cost.

This cold recedes, that pain remains
I'm tossed about between afflictions
The losses accumulate faster than the gains
I know I'm guilty of placing restrictions.

Restrictions upon this infinite soul
A sin of catastrophic proportions
i know my lines, i forgot my role
The mirror of self reveals distortions.

i meditate on omnipotence in silent voice
My eyes open and i light up a smoke
He granted free will for my shitty choice
I'm the punch line, and the fucking joke.

With words i kick the shit out of me
I guess sometimes i just have to bleed
When the swelling goes down i'll be able to see
Spiritual vision will reveal what I need.

The weight of self judgement daily is amassed
from all judgement, Jesus said to refrain
There is no future, over and done is the past
Living *Now* alleviates conditioned pain.

Though our sins be scarlet made white as snow
In a sincere moment of turning
I endeavor to remain open to the flow
Like a child I'm still learning.

And they shall all be taught of God
A biblical quote, prophetic and true
Amongst the crystal walks this clod
Yet, in Her, all things are made new.

ॐ

*

So, you think truth can be *used*
You absurd, arrogant little fool
If it can be thought, it can be abused
You think I Am just some handy tool?

You have learned much, and don't know shit
You would do better to just chop off your head

With so much matter gone, maybe some spirit would
fit
And if not, you'd just be dead.

There you go again, another *concept* accepted
As God asked Adam, "Who told thee"
By the visibility of matter, spirit is not affected
Though formless, I Am *is* always me.

What is my *concept* when I say I?
Is it David, or something most grand?
What is compelling me, why ask why?
I want to know, not understand.

I feel what compels me, it has no voice
Still, it resonates as my very soul
I would probably ignore it if i had a choice
Yet, my purpose, already penned on It's scroll.

Why concepts, a purpose do they serve?
Where we dwell we surely must know
Never again shall i elicit "you have some nerve"
What we plant is what we will grow.

ॐ

Until such time as God sees fit to grace me
with some light, I will just content myself with being a
beholder, using my time to pen the words given me. If
I am still enough to be a crystal clear transparency,
then certainly it is only to be the conduit to transmit it
outward. For God, no matter what some would have
you believe, does not play favorites. We are all the
chosen ones!

So, why is there anything significant about my story? Because, "my" story is your story; we all have a story. We are all spiritual beings sharing a human experience by virtue of the fact that humanly we are all made of the exact same stuff.

Be your appearance dark as polished ebony
Some might say i'm pigment impaired
Wear it proud in harmony
Our Mother designs with flair.

ॐ

The next section has been with me for a while. It had been tapping lightly at the door of consciousness. Yet, when I would open the door it would vanish with the stealth of a specter. A little game of ring and run. No worries, I love how consciousness plays. Not too long ago the door of consciousness opened and in it came, demanding attention. This announcement set my feet firmly on the path of writing this book. As is my way, I say thank you, now please get out of my head and go to the page.

Chapter Two: Who Am "My" ?
(Say it aloud quickly.)

If you voice the question aloud quickly, it is a query that the vast majority of us have asked ourselves at some point in our life. By exploring the question as it is written, it transforms into a question with profound implications with regard to your being introduced to your "real" self. For many of you this will be a very odd, completely new and quite possibly perplexing way in which to regard yourself. In order for us to begin our exploration, I would like to begin with another question. Granted this question will not seem to have a spiritual component, yet it will provide us with a foundation upon which to build.

In your mind's eye, or "for real" if you prefer, I would ask you to go to your window and look out at that shiny *thing* in the driveway or on the street. What is that? You answer, "my" car. And what is a car, but a way to get from point A to point B? So, what is it? "My" transportation.

Now, Slowly turn and scan your surroundings and what do you see? "My" stuff. Amongst "my" stuff is a full length mirror. If you would be so kind as to please stand in front of the mirror. What is that? "Duh, that's me." you answer with sarcasm. In a literal sense that is your body, but let us explore this perception of "me" a little deeper. Please look down and wiggle, what is that? "My" toes which are attached to "my" feet.

Same body in the same mirror, yet because we are assessing smaller parts of the whole, when I ask, "What is that?" You didn't say "me," you said "my."

We can go slowly upward through every body part and at no point will you label that body part other than "my" heart, "my" hip, "my" liver, "my" lungs, "my" shoulder, "my" neck, "my" skull. But, alas, you reach the brain and the ghost of Descartes whispers "I think therefore I am" and with assurance you say, "Okay, found it, that's me." Our command center certainly, the most wondrous computer ever designed, no doubt. But, still the only true answer is "my" brain. And no offense René, but in my humble opinion that is exactly backwards. "I Am therefore I can think" is the truth of being.

So, we've established that the "real" you, can not be located at any specific place in the body. We know that a whole is made from the sum of its parts. Thereby establishing that you are not your body. That body belongs to you. It is "my" body. "My" vehicle, I animate it. I have asked you several poignant questions thus far and now I will ask you the most important question. Who is this "MY" that your body and everything in your world belongs to?

In the beginning of this heading, I asked you to say it aloud quickly. Did you notice what happened? "My" became I. I *is* the truth of being. I *is* "my" identity. Because I *is,* i can voice the most profound truth, I Am, and what pray tell is I Am?

I Am *is* spirit/consciousness.

I Am

This body is not me
This body is I's possession
Though I use these eyes to see
They behold an untrue confession.

I use these feet to walk
Yet, they must go where I does direct

I use this mouth to talk
Of itself can it speak disrespect?

These hands do woodwork precise
Through the years quite a collection
Without I they could never suffice
What does matter know of perfection?

These ears hear multitudes of vibration
Whether wretched or of beautiful voice
The eardrum only knows sensation
It is I that makes the choice.

This brain is always engaged
Wide awake or sound asleep
This soothes, this makes me enraged
The human animal is not very deep.

I'm confused I call myself I
What the hell is that in the mirror?
The reality of body, am I to deny?
Does not ponderance make things clearer?

As it soars does the bird know of air?
Does the fish know of the ocean?
I'm certain neither does care
Just being, without any notion.

Are these just the queries of a fool?
Reality must be touched and seen
Shall I live by humanity's rule?
Will anyone understand what I mean?

This body is not unreal
Unreality, born of perception
Eternality we shall never feel

With a self that began at conception.

This body is His temple, verily
Just keep it physically and spiritually clean
It may ache, but not all to terribly
If I stay grounded in the mystical scene.

So, let me live, yet not i
Let the Spirit lead the way
Let me accomplish, yet not try
I am a beholder of His day.

Like any tool, this body I use
I animate it, it is mine
Most read the paper, watch the news
I am informed by an inward sign.

When I encounter a person on the street
Please give me the wisdom to see the Source
Negating form the true I, I meet
Recognition of spirit is nature's course.

Relax, accept and just exist
Seek The Truth behind the physical seeing
For most a very strange twist
To view the essence of the being.

So, I will see with my heart
I will endeavor to listen with my Soul
I seek only to fulfill my part
I will exist as Being, whole.

ॐ

If I was to suffer a brain trauma and become afflicted with total amnesia, would I still have access to truth? I have no name, no memories, no family, no sense at all of who I am!

The answer is a resounding yes. But, how can that be? You recall nothing; any truth you may have known is gone like dust in the wind. Yet, I have gratitude in my heart.

My eyes are open and even though I remember nothing, if consciously aware of being, then the only thing I can possibly know for certain is, I AM. If I know that I Am, then I can once again come under the care of the universal mind, God, Yahweh, Shiva, Allah, Jehovah, Big guy, Guru, whatever, the semantics matter not.

My search had always been one of a strictly esoteric nature. However, the following quote by **Max Planck,** one of the fathers of quantum theory and one of the most profound thinkers and scientists of the twentieth century states clearly that science and spirit are not so far apart.

"All matter originates and exists only by virtue of a force which brings the particle of an atom to vibration and holds this most minute solar system of the atom together. We must assume behind this force the existence of a conscious and intelligent mind. This mind is the matrix of all matter."

A matrix as defined by Merriam Webster is; "something within or from which something else originates, develops, or takes form."

There are as many paths as there are people, yet we all became in the same way. We live our lives in a billion different ways, doing our best to exist as separate entities, yet this Omniscient, Omnipotent, Omnipresent matrix permeates and wraps itself around everything and allows all the wonders that seemingly exist separately to mesh seamlessly and create the exquisite whole.

I am not so grand as thee
You are not so meek as me
deep rooted and stately, you are akin to the tree
I am synchronicity and flow, akin to the sea.

I do well amongst the cloud
You dwell not under any shroud
You have need to display it proud
I've no need to be so loud.

I am one of a quiet reliance
To spiritual law you stand in defiance
Your resolve comes from conformity and compliance
I lean more toward a cosmic alliance.

I am not wrong, still you are not right
You are saying it's cause to fight
You have eyes, yet they're shut tight
My vision beholden, spiritual sight.

I commune with the fragrant flower
You are hid in your ivory tower
You do love to display your power
I languidly bask, warm spring shower.

I do despise playing the game
You do despise my demeanor tame
Like a moth drawn to a flame
I am drawn to you, we are one... The same.

ॐ

I was in doubt, my knowing quite shoddy
Both Anthony and i got incredibly sick
It's been a long time since i've had an ill body
I wallowed in doubt and it happened that quick.

i know nothing except for what God does teach
i had not a clue where to find the school
Whatever I knew escaped through the breach
closing when I remembered, the only rule.

With our Father I am one
No matter the concept, this is always true
Even in the searing depths He will not shun
No matter where i am, no matter what i do.

There is one word where the secret does lye
Said unconsciously by everyone, every day
It's not a concept, it's the name upon high
In this innocuous word is the way.

Those of you who know will inwardly smile
Those who don't can't believe there's some magical
word
The most tremendous journey, nary a mile
It is within where I must be heard.

I ask only, Father speak this word please
I entertain no concepts, I need not know why
In the depths of humility, upon my knees
You pray through me, I hear you say, I.

ॐ

The recognition that I Am I, as with every important revelation I was blessed with, came just when I needed it. In the early 2000's a compassionate, well intentioned doctor thought he was handing me a prescription for percocet. What he actually handed me was a double edged blade. I say this because, by this point, agony was my constant companion 24/7 and it was worse than intolerable. The percocet made the physical pain tolerable… almost. Yet, spiritually I suffered. Here I am endeavoring to walk this spiritual path, all the while unsteady in a narcotic stupor. The physical toll my professional life was taking was a catalyst for my quickly becoming dependent. I will reiterate, twisted dichotomy. Right after my morning meditation and prayer I would throw down two percocet as soon as I got to the kitchen; gonna be another brutal day.

These next two were written while I was being shown who I Am. They were each a blessing in their own right, but together in short succession they allowed me to acknowledge who I AM, and accept "my" current circumstances with the positive energy and spiritual assurance necessary to overcome anything that life throws at you.

I is a feeling deep inside
It washes over me like the tide
More exhilarating than any ride
The absolute rush of being still.

Saturated completely, yet I thirst
So overfilled I just might burst
Her Grace, my sustenance, always first
I could write for years and not do justice.

My hunger started as a need for healing
My body was broken, my head reeling
Of love i had lost all feeling
A fatalistic zombie, my gun near at hand

Copious amounts of drugs quelled not the pain
Truly on the verge of going insane
A quick fix, one bullet to the brain
My family, Her Grace bestowed.

Like an infirmed newborn, tenderly fed
To the path I was lovingly led
Bruised and battered She cradled my head
Ever so gently, She started to lift.

No judgement, not even a reprimand
Just support, so again I could stand
The fire of life was being fanned
I turned my face to this gentle breeze.

I now dwell constantly in the secret place
A tranquil existence amidst this race
Many do comment of the peace on my face
Do i even comprehend the source?

They say "wow, you look great"
Then adding "have you lost weight"
Looking good, although time is getting late
Within me I hide the pearl.

I use not eyes for this seeing
From mortal sense, I am fleeing
I Am is not form, it is pure being
I seek only what is eternally within.

Forget the body, She healed my soul
In life's epic play a divine role
I Am yours with my being whole
Mere words, but Thank you Mother.

ॐ

I perceived oxy as the only way to cope
Through the wretched shroud of agony,
I could perceive no hope
Grinding 12 hours again tomorrow,
I need more dope
If I can't quell this pain,
I might fashion a rope.

It was truly horrific
When Suicidal Thoughts began
From them, from pain,
from everything I ran
I can't live like this
Broken shell of the man
I can tolerate no more,
"oh yes you can."

With Supreme Grace
The Lord's voice did resonate
I will grant you relief
from the pain to which you're prostrate
I am love, I am life,
I Am Your Fate
Come dwell in my mansions,
Your needs I will sate.

Father, how can I enter?
When religion I abhor

My Heart melted,
He just opened the door
So I stepped through
Not knowing what's in store
My child of Your Love
Is all I implore.

He made no demands
of religious belief
My label meant naught
In his relief
His angels bore me up
He shouldered my grief
Before awestruck eyes
He turned over that leaf.

My body, his Temple,
Proof Miracles exist
It's been quite some time
Since my anger's made a fist
Love and grace overwhelmed me
I cared not to resist.
For a supposed agnostic
Surely a strange twist.

So, now I Daily wake
To the ultimate High
Cradled in love so pure
It brings tears to the eye
God Eternal, within,
Not up in the sky
I can again face the mirror
I like this guy.

ॐ

Chapter Three: Gratitude

With gratitude being the core principle of my spiritual existence, I must say thank you to you, my open, adventurous spiritual seekers. I always felt that if "my" writing (a very loose interpretation) had any value to anyone other than myself, that those of my spiritual household would find it. If you find anything in this book that stokes your fire, then you can be grateful to a dear friend of mine who shamed me into action by telling me that i was selfish for not sharing my writing (you know who you are, Juliette).

My writing is deeply personal and deeply profound (to me), and I had never intended it for public consumption. As joyous and fulfilling as it is to live a Spiritual life of gratitude, this path is not an easy one. I endeavor to practice the presence (akin to Buddhist mindfulness) to the best of my ability. Which means that I acknowledge and thank The Source every day in every way. Sounds simple enough, right?

Try this little test. Today, whether eating or drinking, before anything passes your lips, say Thank you. You will do it many times, but I guarantee at some point you will start chewing or drinking and then think, "oh man, I forgot to say thank you." Once you seek The Light, your drab little world brightens up a bit and light filters into those dark places.

For me this took the form of much greater self awareness leading me to truly comprehend how far short i was from moving forward, actually, upward toward my goal of Conscious union with Our Source. Which led me to write what I affectionately titled Thank you from a shit head.

*

Thank you Father, thank you much
I'll catch you when again i'm in need
I was numb until your touch
Only becoming fertile when you planted your seed.

It's so amazing to again feel great
I've decided to walk in your way
I'm feeling burdened will you bear the weight
I'll step up the amount that i pray.

Jesus promised he would take up my yoke
First let me calculate the minimum cost
I'll get right to it, just one more toke
Walking backwards, a sure way to get lost.

How could i lose sight of what He's shown
Is my vision really that blurred
My reliance on the corporeal again has grown
The penalties i have again incurred.

Full of doubt as Thomas was once
These human eyes are not to be believed
Yet, to doubt the Soul takes a real dunce
The heart knows when truth is received.

The battle with duality i am losing
Every morning i claim one power
My choices are shit, why am i choosing
Not to bask in the Spirits shower.

In God's Spirit liberty is found
Please God, give me a swift kick in the ass
Because You Are, this spot is holy ground
By your grace will the narrow gate I pass.

Perfect what concerneth, perform the appointed
Make my only concern knowing you aright
With thine single eye no longer disjointed
I only shine when you are my light.

I certainly did not choose this path
Thy grace chose it for me
God plus me equals one, loves math
As Paul said, "let it be"

My mind stayed on Thee, bestows thy peace
Let the world know not how I am fed
The good shepherd warms me, let me gift my fleece
Let me dwell in the heart, not the head.

Evil and good both projections of the mind
Let me dwell in thy divine space
Get busy searching, be still and find
My heart restless, until I repose in thy grace.

ॐ

*I feel it within, the words are flowing
If I don't stop now, I'll just keep going
The basic premise of what my poetry is showing
Within is this bud and it is growing
The flower that blooms is one of knowing
You'll see it in the eyes, they'll be glowing
The continuum of now birthed from nows sowing
For corporeal wares I shall not be ho-ing
This opportunity to share, I shall not be foregoing
I hope you enjoyed the read as much as I did the write
It's late and I'm sleepy, I bid you goodnight.*

ॐ

For the new day and every word that I write I have
deep gratitude, and I consciously choose to say thank
you often.

Thankful for this
Thankful for that
My apologies Father
I got lazy and fat.

Thankful for Soul
Thankful for Spirit
Thank you Mother
For the ability to hear it.

Thankful for life
Thankful for love
Thank you my brother Jesus
Peace of the dove.

Thankful for truth and
The innate gift to know
Thank you for the universe
I am synchronicity and flow.

ॐ

It is a daunting task to try and categorize my
writing and fit a poem into a particular heading. Many
have multiple, revelatory themes and many go on for
pages. I just follow along wherever I am led. Not all of
my poems of gratitude say thank you up front and out
loud.

The bird sings because it can
It sounds like joy's release
The master composer wrote the tune
Soulful and compelling in its peace.

The perpetual march of the sea
The ebb and flow of the tide
The rhythm to it is perfection
I can feel it inside.

There is an invisible something
In the stars and in the trees
In the birds and in the flowers
I Am all of these.

In the silence I feel the vibration
The voice of a single minute cell
The chorus of life's unification
A billion harmonize in this shell.

My frequency emits love
Not to a space or in time
It merges with the Source of being
Then flows back as this rhyme.

Profoundly drivel or poetry profound
Just a tweak of conscious perception
In school I cut english most every day
I believe not, it's my brain's conception.

For me writing releases the soul
From the torment of the mortal cage
In gratitude it wings swift and eternal
A blissful dance across this page.

My spirit unites with awe
Which can only mean one thing
In harmony with all of creation
All subject unto One King.

Chapter Four: Family

In my youth I was a bit of a wild child. As my poem states my union with Kathy was of divine proportions. I can confidently state this because not many women as awesome as Kathy would have put up with my hard living ways between the ages of 18-26. However, one fateful day in 1995 after four years of marriage Kathy said those two magic words, "It's blue," and my life was changed for the best! Just knowing you are going to be a parent is like a slap in the face, and I mean that in the best way possible.

For me it was a crazy time. A new state, starting a new business, buying our first home, and the only reason conceivable to take on all that responsibility. Our glorious Nicole.

When Kathy and I took our first lamaze class, I came across a quote that seared itself into my consciousness and has stayed with me every day since. "You only get one chance to create a masterpiece, sculpt carefully."

Father, I seek your guidance
So that I may rightly teach
Let me sow the seeds of love
To the heavens their garden will reach.

Let me till the soil of compassion
A bountiful harvest they will reap
Let me carefully pluck weeds of ignorance
Only the most beautiful flowers to keep.

Please let your light shine through me
As to nourish their awakening soul
Please let your living waters quench

Grow the perfect spirit, whole.

Help me to be a sage teacher
Not a cruel master of tasks
Help me to reveal pure being
The kind that needs no masks.

Please let their yield be plentiful
With hearts that openly share
Let them see you in all things
Making it impossible not to care.

For your grace is always sufficient
To those who are spiritually wise
Let them know oneness with no separation
Please, let them see all with your eyes.

I ask as your adoring son
A parents gift unto Her child
Some lessons require sternness
Still others need only a smile.

ॐ

I dare say do not wait
Chase what is your heart's desire
Do it now, it's never too late
Bow not to the dying of the fire.

Never relinquish your golden dream
It is folly others will say
Keep it polished, let it gleam
This life is your play.

Script it anyway you see fit
Let your role be ever grand
Don't put up with anyone's shit
They never will understand.

They laughed at Edison and Einstein
Two dreamers, two brilliant men
They will expect you to have no spine
The sword, less mighty than the pen.

You must know what I never did
You can accomplish anything, anything at all
No matter a senior or a kid,
never cede the things that enthrall.

For all spirits there is a plan
Your heart's desire *Is* Her will
If you can dream it, Yes you can
This journey is a thrill.

Listen closely, life is calling
Calling you to live your glory
The bold heart is never stalling
It beats the rhythm of an epic story.

Most wake one day to dreams faded
Always meaning to make them come true
Now they're tired, a little jaded
Sadly, away those dreams flew.

Looking to the future is not wrong
But never forget, Now is the only time
In joyous rapture sing your song
Let love pour out in a rhyme.

You go right out and save the world
Let Spirit be you loving guide
Stand tall with your flag unfurled
You must heed what is inside.

People will laugh and condescend
Of their own path they are afraid
Banter not, no need to defend
Your heart is not up for trade.

You might find yourself all alone
For great spirits, a great place to be
The herd always fears the unknown
The Soul will show you to see.

What is past is over and done
Yet, most give regret its rise
Do not lament the setting sun
Again tomorrow it will illumine the skies.

What that means is simply this
Each new day has promise unbound
Live consciously or you might miss
Your inner guide speaks without sound.

ॐ

Nikki was an incredibly mature, amazingly astute little gem with a heart of gold, who was coming of age humanly and spiritually as I was coming of age spiritually. As I said we learned from and taught one another. When you become a parent, you automatically become a teacher. Yet, what I found out was that i am just as much a student as i am a teacher. About the time Nikki was 5 or 6, I asked her if she would like to go to the Thanksgiving food drive with me.

She answered yes, so I explained what it was for and the fact that the food bank can get a lot more food with money than we can. So, I asked her if she wanted to add some of her money to my donation for the food bank.

At the time the most important thing in her world was a trip to Build A Bear with her cousin Anna from New York; for which she had been saving for quite some time. I have no clue what bears cost but at the time she had 17 dollars and change saved. When she handed me her money and I counted it, as is happening now, tears started to well up in my eyes.

"Daddy what's wrong?"

"Nothing sweetheart, i'm just sooo proud of you."

She had given me 14 dollars and change, the lion's share of her savings.

"Sweety, that's almost all of your savings."

"I know daddy, but people need to eat more than I need a bear. I better start saving for next year."

...Yeah sure, I'm the teacher.

A child's eye beholds the wretched
Cynicism clouds not her seeing
She beholds brothers and sisters in purity
She beholds a fellow human being.

Her eye beholds decay and filth
Her purity judges not such state

But for the grace of God
You and I, to suffer like fate.

She asks, "Daddy can we help him?"
"Daddy, something we must do!"
Her eyes behold blessed vision
Her eyes behold what's true.

Even the wretched are His children
Even the lowest to dwell upon high
Hardened heart to break wide open
Of purer eyes was not i.

ॐ

In innocence she smiled
my heart she beguiled
Knowing not the power she possessed
An aire to remain stoic
A feat almost heroic
Of pure love my smile confessed.

Child, sweet dear child
Behavior raucous, so very wild
From moment one our souls did meld
Oh' such sweet pain
She can make me insane
Did she know the power she held?

I think she just may
My heart she does play
Always in the perfect key
Away my anger flies
She bats those big brown eyes
Lord, this kid is working me.

Enough, you've made me mad
You had better listen to dad
She certainly has me riled
Her look infused with love
Bestows grace from above
Truly, in innocence she smiled.

ॐ

In 2001 came my best buddy. Anthony was named after both of my grandfathers, who were also my best buddies. Anthony (Cappy) Ferrari and Anthony (Duke) Maraglino. Lo and behold, he is huge like Duke and a stone cold ball buster like Tony; and me, that apple didn't fall far.

My dad was an enigma. He could quote you Voltaire and then knock you on your ass. Yet, he never hit me. He had this incredibly effective implied threat in his mannerisms. If that didn't work, he would speak quietly and calmly with a finger full of temple hair as he explained the error of your ways while lifting slightly. But, he was from a time when men were men, and that's what they made their sons; especially those that follow in the family footsteps. A true beast in his day, my 70 hour work weeks were only proof that his son lacked grit. Sweet Tony would not be exposed to that outmoded way of child rearing.

Suck it up son, be tough
Learn to be a man
Bitter sting of embarrassment
On emotions thou levied a ban.

Let others see not your weakness

A man goes not around crying
Shield of galvanized facade
We commence the true self to lying.

Father, what is so wrong
With emotions worn on the sleeve
The world is harsh for the weak, son
Surely a pummeling to receive.

Father, why is it known as weakness
To merely display the heart
You will understand when your older, son
It was so from the very start.

Father, do you mean to say
To be a man is all about force
I don't make the rules, son
I merely follow nature's course.

Father, are you trying to tell me
To be a man I must wield power
Father, I say unto you
Nature's course also yielded the flower.

Son, as I said before
I do not make the rules
Father, it sounds unto me
Like misguided fathers propagate fools.

Son, doest thou call me a fool
Of wisdom I have imparted much
Yes, you've imparted vast knowledge
Yet, I've longed for your loving touch.

Son, have I not clothed and fed you
Provided shelter and all that you need

Clothing, shelter and sustenance abound
But why did my soul you not feed.

Son, of soulful things I have heard
But i must say that i don't know much
I will be the pupil, please teach me
Let us start with that loving touch.

ॐ

I would venture to guess that many of us grew up with fathers who were stingy with their love and approval. I was 36 before my dad lost his mind, apparently, and told me he was proud of me and that I was a better contractor than he ever was. It only took 38 years and for us to consume most of a bottle of Johnny Walker Black before he gave me a real hug and told me he loved me. Anth is 18 and he still hugs me for no other reason than that is how we have always expressed affection. I was Anthony's baseball coach for many years, and I have seen many fathers and many sons. It ain't a pretty picture.

I have endeavored to sculpt very carefully; like Michelangelo did with the statue of David, all I did was chip away the erroneous pieces to reveal the glory inherent within. I am not claiming Michelangelo status by any means. Although, I was blessed with a wisdom and an insight that very few possessed, conceited much?

Nope, blessed to have had my 96 year old grandma Rose move in with us for the last 5 years of her life. Yes, that's right, two weeks short of 101. We gave her a 100th birthday bash with all the remaining family. Who gets to do that? Like I said, Blessed.

Now, having a feisty, active, sharp as a tack 98 year old Italian grandma around will teach you patience, something i was never possessed of. And it will give you a perspective that only a hundred years of existence can provide. As you can imagine Rosie had some issues and as such, I as a dutiful grandson and her health proxy spent more time at hospitals than I could stomach. Between Kathy and I, my sister Chris and her husband Mark, there was always someone around to have grandma's back. Which, at the hospital, I saw was not the case for so many of the forgotten elderly patients. Which lead me to write the following:

Labeled, negated and forgotten
To feeble to enrage, the elderly
Like so many apparitions
We see them clearly;
Yet see right through, fierce denial
Our fragile mortality frightened to the core.

How are we so blind
How are we so callous
As to relegate to least of stature
Possessing wisdom we do not
So very willing to impart; life's rush,
Their voice, scattered dust in the wind.

With dogmatic respect we sit
Their words audibly received, still rarely
Ever to be truly heard
They move slow, they talk slow,
They have earned it, sweet reverence
Of the present we look past.

Technology rushes headlong, ever forward

Leaving these gems in the past, great truths
Unchanging, have ever been so.
They have seen, they have done
We all know they tell it straight, why not
Folly, pretense, and aire's long rejected.

In condemnation I write
Of you, of me, of all, the young,
The strong, the supremely impatient
Profound the phrase live and learn
For they have lived, shall we
In the depths of our obtuse vanity
Fail to learn.

Praise due the orient
Cultural respect and reverence, Spiritual knowledge
A diamond truly shines forever.

ॐ

As I journeyed further along the spiritual path, profound yet painful feelings of empathy and compassion began to awaken within me. I have pretty much banished the word hate from my and my children's vocabulary. But, I have to say, I **Hate** hospitals. As hard as I try to stay centered, it always feels as though the energy is being sucked from my being when I'm there. Seeing and hearing all those forgotten souls seeking for help that would be too long in coming, it would have been impossible not to feel sympathy. Yet, I did not. Sympathy says, "oh you poor dear, I feel so sorry for you." To me that has an aire of superiority, like you are above such a base experience. Now, empathy on the other hand, embraces you, looks you in the eye with love and

says, "I understand." I think of this next one as simply,
carnage.

They are falling to my left and to my right
There is carnage about the place I dwell
What *is, is* a knowing, but i still have sight
My human eyes behold my other self's hell.

Though peripheral, it strikes at my center
My secret place encased in the light
Where pure being resides, it shall not enter
I still experience this queasy knot in spite.

My oneness with God is my oneness with all
For me, the place anguish can arise
After years on the path, my knowing so small
I seemingly can do nothing to assuage their cries.

What does it take Father, i'm on my knees
I pray you, show me what am I to do
With all the consciousness i'm able, I ask please
<u>You</u> called me, I<u> didn't</u> call you!

You would not have chosen me without reason
Do tell, I would dearly love to know
Please forgive me if my tone sounds like treason
I only desire to be a conduit for your flow.

Am I still looking through that glass so dark
Is my knowing even a minuscule grain
Is my presumption of looming light, a lark
The physical torture i endured compares not to that
pain.

Shall I study harder, meditate more
It seems most often I ponder thy grace

You know my heart, my motives that of a whore?
Tell me!, how do I dwell in your space?
How many more layers must I peel away?
Until illusion is dispelled for evermore
Grant me the stillness to do as you say
Your greatest son said to knock upon thy door.

Though my knuckles be sore, i'll bang till they bleed
Then I will gladly switch to the other hand
This hunger of my soul only you can feed
My limited knowing says you won't give me sand.

So, here I am Father, meek, completely bare
One with all, yet so utterly alone
A lost voyager I send up a flare
Just awaiting, for the way to be shown.

You have shown me your love and also your peace
My humanness still puts me to the test
Please Father, help me, make it to cease
Every word I write, my love for thee confessed.

ॐ

Now on to my muse, Kathleen, who would most likely not be a part of this story without grandma Rose. Their places in my life and on my spiritual journey are so interwoven that the compassion and empathy that I poured out in 'carnage' was also for my beloved.

You see, Kathy has Lupus, an autoimmune disease that can have devastating effects on various major systems in the body. I live with Kathy and I would be loath to describe it in detail. So, to say it is misunderstood by the general public is an understatement, and from what I've seen the doctors don't have a great handle on it either.

There have been times that i have, in confusion and frustration lashed out, as i sort of did in 'carnage'. However, the Father that Jesus taught me of is one of love, mercy and forgiveness, so I have no fear of reprisal. God would not have granted me freedom of expression, when knowing David, He knew I would fully express myself.

I can feel it, it's building inside
This anger wants to burst
I will not submit, I will not hide
Father, for you, I hunger and thirst.

I didn't choose you, You chose me
So, now I demand to know why
Why didn't you just let me be
At least then i could still beseech to the sky.

Yet, that is an option no longer
I can only seek what I already am
In your care I have never been stronger
Still, these waters rage against the dam.

Your omniscient hand has guided this knowing
Things of which I never dreamed existed
So, why is it i am not showing
Why am i still so Damn twisted?

Except for the highly enlightened few
The world would say I'm in denial
Your omniscience has shown what's true
Still, i feel as though I'm on trial.

The death sentence of unenlightenment, largely
looming
In the silence you whisper in my ear
The voice of ignorance is outside booming
That wretched voice resonates with fear.

I just don't know what you want from me
It seems hell, this lowly foul place
You gave me eyes, please let me see
Let mine eyes gaze upon thy face.

ॐ

I was friends with her brothers, and met Kathy shortly after we moved from the Bronx to Long Island when I was 8 years old. We had taken a family vacation and grandma Rose fell in love with East Quogue, a sleepy little town on the eastern end of Long island. Shortly thereafter she convinced my grandpa to move there. Our family followed suit within two years, building a new house just blocks from Rosie, who had chosen a neighborhood with a house literally a stones throw from where Kathy lived.

So, in essence if it wasn't for grandma, I in all likelihood would never have met Kathy. Rosie had no idea that in 1970 life's synchronicity was facilitating her best friend and caregiver for the last five years of her life. Although I did everything I could do, Kathy bore the brunt of doing the things a 98 year old woman needs help with. Babe, you're an angel.

Sometimes when thoughts come to me and I start writing I get swept up in the flow of how good it sounds in my head and I just flow first word to last. Then I will go back over it and think, "man, that was way easier to write than to read." This next one falls into the category of: this is either really good… or not. You tell me if I should have put it in the 'not all winners section.

I must have been under
An angels grace, etherial face
Yes, I will be your wife
I need not some made up
Hallmark holiday, this day
To know your my love, my life
To bestow what the heart does say, every day
It continues to expand; just look
into the souls window, my eyes
And understand always
The withering of time it defies
Now and forever, you are the owner
Of my heart from the start
Eternally soul love never dies.

ॐ

I sure do despise buying cards as Kathy knows, it's kind of our running joke.

Once again a card I forsake
Gee, what a surprise
I certainly have no need to pay
For something said best with the eyes.

I write words that forever profess
The unspoken emanation of my soul
Our love dominates my being
Without ever exerting control.

Such profound freedom in this unity
Love's bond has no need of chains
Two spirits unique with one destiny
While neither one holds any reins.

You always let me be just who I am
Even when i was a dick
My evolution fueled by your flame
Always, my cool, sexy, green eyed chick.

Our path guided by the divine hand
Could there be any other way to explain
The two amazing children we were blessed with
I will savor every moment that remains

There never could have been any other
My being cold without the brilliance of its sun
Such light and warmth nourish my growth
For me you're the only one.

ॐ

It would not be possible to tell my spiritual story without including my sister Christine, who has been a huge part of my story since day one. As many siblings are, Chris and I were partners in crime from the outset. Actually not so much partners as mastermind and fall guy. As an older good girl sibling with a sketchy younger brother her transparent deflections of blame were not so transparent to my parents. I was as a youth, shall we say, husky. A fact that Chris made frequent use of for her twisted amusement, something my parents seemed not to care about. So, it was I who got in trouble when I lashed out in self defense.

As polar opposites who were quite often quarrelsome with each other common ground has not always been easy to find. Yet, when I stand my ground I never look to find Chris. For agree with me or not I know she will always be right behind me. Chris has always had my back. From our early days when she would make sure Regina didn't sneak me, as I did battle with her brother Louie on a Bronx playground. To more recent times when she convinced me of the prudence and then helped to make it financially feasible for me to keep a medical insurance policy that carried the monetary weight of a mortgage payment. I dare not even ponder my current situation had Chris not interceded. Long ago as little kids Chris and I cultivated a pristine little patch of ground that would forever be the perfect size for us to stand upon; Love and Loyalty. However, there is one more thing I would ask of you my dear sister, next time around instead of watching, laughing and waiting to run and narc, Please just wake me up before I pee in the refrigerator.

Age matter not, it pales and falls from view
Boundless spirit knows not time nor space
Yet, it takes the wisdom of a sage
To see past the past, the mortal mesmerism of age
You are timeless beauty, style and grace.

A calendar can not define what is divine, eternal
You always were, you always will be
Your being has blessed my soul
In our unity I am whole
For this truth I need not eyes to see.

Like attracts like is a cosmic law
We were, and will be together for all time

With no beginning or end
No power could rend
One in consciousness, a relationship sublime.

In this incarnation, you are my sister
Past or present, who is to say
However, one thing I know
Our love will continually grow
I love you, Happy Birthday.

ॐ

It's not only Kathy who is in on the I don't buy cards joke. This next one I really had no place for, but it makes me smile every time I read it. I'm sure some of my beach lovers can relate. Being that I was at Christine's newly acquired beach house in Long Island when I wrote it, I figured I could shoehorn it in here.

I walk along the sole trodden path
High above, the tern arcs and swerves
I incur nature's paternal wrath
This is my home, you have some nerve
The thought you did neglect, I will protect
You are far too close to my nest
From such trespass I quickly sped
All the while ducking my head
Awesome instincts, I was really quite impressed.

To an onlooker, a hysterical sight
Running, swinging, my towel in defiance
God's creature of superior intellect and might
From a mere beach tern, fleeing in compliance
As a general rule, I play not the fool

Yet, nature's so adept at leveling the field
Their screams said, "run boy run"
I could swear they were having fun

Purposeful power infused with speed did they wield.
With great relief, I finally made the waters edge
They eyed me carefully, patrolling the sky
Whenever I would venture the dune's sandy ledge
They would descend from upon high
This was not fun, I had to make a run
Later, being more tiresome than soon
Towel flailing, off I did go
Was anyone, privy to the show
It's so enlightening to be the buffoon.

ॐ

Christine helped facilitate my spiritual story by marrying Mark Tobin. Mark became the brother I never had, as we raised our families together. My nephew Matthew (Dudesy) came shortly after Nikki, and my niece Isabella (Belle) was born shortly after Anth. I have to say sorry bro, I never wrote a poem about you. However I will tell the readers a little about you. Mark is a life of the party guy, one of those people who can take center stage and command an audience. Yet, to describe such a multi faceted personality is a precarious task.

So, bro I got that look in my eye and my Bronx, Italian wiseass wants to come out, but in a loving way. My brother is a walking oxymoron. He is a spiritual capitalist, a beer swilling oenophile, a burger chomping gourmet chef, a compassionate hedonist, an upwardly mobile longshoreman; I saved the most contrasting for last, a righteous lawyer. When he is not doing battle with the government to protect the property rights of the individual, he is a winemaker extraordinaire! And because I have no oxymoronic counterpart, I'll just say it, generous to a fault. Not to mention a husband, father and friend.

For purposes of this story though, Mark's best quality is the fact that he introduced me to the family patriarch, his father Herb. Herb is one of the principles of a foundation that disseminates the work of Joel S. Goldsmith, the founder of *The Infinite Way*. I was doing some work for Herb in his office and walked into a storage closet and without realizing it, my life was about to be changed forever. Floor to ceiling books, the compiled teachings of the preeminent mystic and spiritual teacher of the twentieth century Joel S. Goldsmith.

The first book to catch my eye was *The Art of Meditation*, which I read that night and started practicing in the morning. It is a relatively short book and meditation is patience and practice not rocket science. The second book to catch my eye was *Spiritual Healing*. Oh, now this is what I need, to heal my ailing body. Silly, silly boy. Through the years Herb provided me with a great deal of the reading material I required to stoke my spiritual fire, which started with a small spark and has continued to increase in intensity up until today.

This really could have been written under the dedication or the gratitude heading because when Chris became a Tobin, my life took an upward path. Yet, It goes so much deeper than just providing access to reading material. Herb and his amazing wife Fran basically adopted us and became our Florida family. It is with all love and gratitude that I thank Herb and Fran and the whole Tobin clan.

Being under the family heading still, I would like to share something I wrote about two of the most loving, giving, caring, beautiful spirits I have ever known. As I told you I write what I feel and although this may be an inflammatory subject, I really couldn't care less. I don't remember what set me off, I just remember being highly annoyed when I wrote it.

Well okay, I do remember, but this is not about having a pissing contest with the "God hates fags" sub human rejects who were all over the media at the time. Let's face it, many of us have a family member or friend that is gay; if not in the nuclear than in the extended. The idea that there are those who wallow in the thought process that could put together a tag line as offensive, disgusting and ultimately contradictory as that is mind boggling to me. Love you cuz.

*

How is it love is wrong
The heart rejoices in love's song
How does the zealot come to believe
That it's wrong for Paul to love Steve
Viewing life through hateful eyes
So much so that they come to despise
The blessed union of two like souls
Who gives a shit, marital roles
What God ordains no man shall smite
For love pertains to what is right.

ॐ

Conspicuously missing is mention of my mother, Lillian. Lil was a cool chick with a ready laugh accompanied by a hysterical snort, a huge heart full of love, a sharp wit and the sometimes heavy handed manner of an Italian mom. She battled cancer for about three years past the five they originally said would be miraculous. This proved a most difficult time to find the quiet, receptive, at peace state of mind that I was getting used to as my norm. As such the flow of writing dried up. The only way a flowing river gets blocked is if a dam is erected. Fear, Doubt, Uncertainty, limitation… I let them into my secret place… DAMN!!

*

Is it possible
For the well to run dry
Arid and deplete
In hell did i cry.

Once completely sated
Is it any longer so
Am I any longer fated
I need the stronger flow.

Reading what is written
I do perceive it is shit
I'm just not allowing
Am I any longer fit?

My perception is not wrong
This does truly blow
Just mental masterbation
And it does truly show.

I know what must be done
I must put up my pen
Wait until I am called
For it is only then
That!!

T.G.I.M.S.

ॐ

    T.G.I.M.S. is how I end everything that I write. I didn't do it in this book because I didn't want to be redundant. It is not usually a part of the poem. However, it was an appropriate end to this one. It stands for Thy Grace Is My Sufficiency. It is so much a part of my being that I have it tattooed over my heart. The T is in the shape of a wishbone, a loving shout out counterpart to Nikki's and all the wishbones I made sure snapped in her favor as a child.

Hello old friend, it's been some time
I think I needed a break for a while
My pen had lost the rhythm to it's rhyme
Immersed in verse, yet devoid of a smile.

Mom's passing exacted a toll
On many days I felt the empty space
I would truly feel the rift in my soul
I could hear her voice and see her face.

Was I a victim to tricks of the mind
Could I really be hearing and seeing
I did seek, but was I ready to find
Life's connection in pure being.

Once abundant meter did not flow
The pathway of such had been blocked
The winds of change sure did blow
The door to my heart, chained and locked.

It had to be locked, love to retain

If not, our bond be forever lost
Denial and rigidity a sure path to pain
This knowing would not count the cost.

In unity with God through meditation
Each day my prayers grew stronger
No mortal bond can last the duration
Love, yes, but I shall grieve no longer.

For many months my hand had been lame
It was again longing for the feel of the page
Pick me up, it would call my name
Let go of all the lingering rage.

Mom's passing was a torturous test
Not of faith, but rather of knowing
It tried like hell to get my best
Yet truth, kept right on showing.

My mind did see and my spirit did hear
This was not a mere trick of the senses
In letting go, I lost not what was dear
The soul sense always recompenses.

I do not believe we end at the grave
Nor do I believe conception is where we start
I will no longer dwell in an emotional cave
We were not meant to pay that part.

ॐ

To be perfectly honest, I had no intention of writing of the passing of my parents. Most is too personal and way heavier than the tone of this book.

Hey, you said perfectly honest. O.K. those are mine, and my children's when i pass, and I could never get through putting it to the page, again! However, I brought you here, and anyone who has ever lost someone to a horrible disease will be able to relate to my cathartic outpouring.

One day I walked into mom's house while she was in the kitchen and she didn't hear me come in. When she turned and saw me, she screamed and dropped her water glass, which cracked me up. Mom was not amused, which made me laugh that much harder. From that point on whenever I would walk into the house I would loudly shout, "Yo, Lil" and wherever she was she would shout back, "Yo, Dave." The first time I walked into the house after she passed I shouted, "Yo, Lil" just because… Then I grabbed a pen and the closest writing surface, an empty QVC box (mom's crack the last couple years) and wrote this.

*

Yo, Lil
Be at peace
Not one more Fucking pill
Enjoy your release.

With dignity and grace
The battle you did wage
Bask in God's infinite space
Free of mortalities cage.

Peace descends
Release all care
Blissful charms in the everlasting arms
In Oneness I will see you there!

ॐ

Chapter Five: Something In The Water

Of all my friends who became couples in high school, including Kathy and I, seven of us have laughed in the face of the divorce statistics. One such couple is Danny and Patty. I met Danny when I got to middle school, nope wrong, in our day it was jr. high, and we have been friends for more than forty years. I met Patty in Mr. Hubbard's 9th grade social studies class. Our lifelong friendship was sealed one day when, being the hot blooded Italian that I am, I leaned back in my desk and let Patty put her frozen milquetoast fingers under my arms to get warm. Thank God for my Lacoste velour shirt, those were some cold digits (go ahead and laugh at my velour. If you are my contemporary, you had one too!).

Patty and I went out for about a minute at some point. However, we realized immediately that there was nothing more than friendship between us and we have remained friends to this day. If you walk the spiritual path with your eyes and ears open and receptive it begins to dawn on you that all those little coincidences are actually not random at all. They are universal synchronicities, playing out the cosmic law of like attracts like.

We are energy beings, as such we all emit a frequency from our electrical discharge. As is the case with tuning forks; if you vibrate one, any other tuning fork in the general vicinity which is tuned at the same frequency will start to vibrate due to harmonic resonance. We have all heard of the aura, the electrical coronal discharge surrounding humans. This electrical discharge can be documented using kirlian photography. This electrical field permeates, surrounds and forms a visible field around us that meets, mingles and informs all the other fields that we encounter. Hocus pocus you say. Want to see??

Try this little experiment: sit in front of a blank white or light colored wall, hold your hands eye level, palms facing you, fingertips a couple inches apart or so. Now focus intently on the whole picture, but stare at nothing specifically. Yes your hands are prominent, but focus on the whole picture. Breath deep and slow. Within a short period your awareness will slowly move to the only visual stimulation and you will begin to see fuzzy rings of energy outlining your fingertips. At this point it is ok to focus a little bit on your fingers, but please don't stare. This is just as much an awareness, as it is a visual happening. Once you are clearly seeing your energy you can merge it with your other fingers and have some fun bending and warping it.

The same holds true for humans, as with tuning forks. Our friends, and the loved ones we choose to spend time with, are people who resonate with a like frequency. So, it is easy, comfortable, and natural feeling to be with them. You'll notice I said choose to be with. In an extended family situation there will most likely be someone you don't truly resonate with, yet don't forget, if your frequencies weren't somewhat similar, you probably wouldn't be seeing each other at Thanksgiving. So, endeavor to see the truth behind the mask.

Strolling down the street I smile at you
You walk by indifferent, the gift unreturned
This has occurred maybe a thousand times
You think by now I would have learned.

I pass through a door, holding it open for you
You walk past brusquely, as if it's expected

I reject the desire to curtly say "you're welcome"
For so many, common courtesy rejected.

In maddening traffic I yield to let you in
The next tired driver gets your blaring horn
As if the space your car occupies is sacred
Facilitate my delay, receive my scorn.

But then a pure soul smiles back at me
In sincerity, you meet my eyes and say "thank you"
You let the next beleaguered driver into your lane
Then again I remember why it is I love you.

ॐ

A short ways into my journey I was feeling a little lost
and solitary.

I feel like a stranger in a strange land
Pondering truths of which so few understand
As they sedate themselves with entertainment, inane
Blessed impartation, the pearl of great price
I want to share, but to know must suffice
If I told them they'd think me insane.

Am I the only one who sees God everywhere
No i'm not napping, I am in prayer
Seeking union through a constant realization
It's not about religion, it's all about spirit
If you desire the contact, you must be near it
I care not for the ritual of the presentation.

I touch God at sunrise sitting on Her beach
But you must go to church, the dogmatists beseech
Can you not understand that I do

How can I possibly find, if I don't seek
I can not explore infinity just one day a week
I AM the essence of what's true.

Everyone worships how they see best
The illumined have shown that the fruitage is the test
I pray your bushels are overflowing
For me the sweetest fruit comes directly from the vine
A succulence and sweetness that is truly divine
I seek a consciousness worthy for the growing.

ॐ

I was still in the world, but not really of it any longer. As such I had no one to discuss my spiritual journey with, which is exactly when a major synchronicity in my life was revealed. I was in my home town where it is not unusual to run into old friends and family. I had seen Danny's father Bruce two days in a row, but both times the parking lot situation did not allow for me to stop. For some reason that I couldn't quite grasp, the rest of the day my self judgement was telling me, 'You've known him since you were a kid, you should have made the effort dirtbag.' The third day in a row that I saw him, the message finally permeated my thick skull and I knew that we needed to speak.

So I parked, jumped out and walked over to Bruce. We caught up and then as we were parting, almost as an afterthought, Bruce said,

"Oh by the way, you know that Danny and Patty bought a house out here?"

"Really? No I didn't."

He gave me the address, we shook hands and parted. As is so often the case, our group of friends had scattered into our various lives and hadn't been in touch in too many years. Anxious to see old friends, I immediately drove to their house. I walked up and surprised them sitting on the beach.

Not knowing that my spiritual life was about to change, my heart was still elated at seeing such dear friends again. After talking and laughing for a while, another friend asked Patty a question. When she answered, my spirit soared; for there was no doubt, the words she spoke and the way she spoke them let me know immediately that she was traversing the same path as I was and that those two paths just converged. Believe it or not, it is hard for me to put into words just how vital to my spiritual growth it was to find a spiritual confidant, who also happened to be a very dear friend. Just another case of me getting exactly what I needed, when I needed it. As is so often the case my awareness came in the form of the written word.

Thank you again, my flame you have fanned
My very dear friend
No explanations you just understand
My spirit you gently tend
Our harmonious flow allows me to grow
I feel at one with your being
You knew my heart
right from the start
At first, I knew not what I was seeing.

28 years ago I had only human sight
Your beauty was so very appealing

28 years later I discern your true light
The source of Your beauty, soul revealing
Though your fingers were freezing, the connection
pleasing
As you put milquetoast under my arms
I thought it quite quizzical
The connection not physical
For a girl with such obvious charms.

We knew not of the path we would walk
We were just kids without a clue
Time apart mattered not, as we started to talk
A stagnant friendship, now fresh and new
Learning of the word, it was then I heard
A friend speak the words of the soul
You could call it a connection
More so a reflection
Both chosen for the very same role

No longer was it bottled up inside
I thought I would go insane
No longer did I have to hide
No longer did I have to fein
You made no joke of the truth I spoke
It was a truly joyous release
There was no surprise
In your knowing eyes
What I saw was My peace.

The kind of peace that comes only
From a heart touched by Her love
No longer was I spiritually lonely
We could help each other rise above
I know God is near when I hear
You finish my very same thought
We both had a need

The spirit now freed
A gift that could never be bought.

Looking back there is only one
Person who I could ever have guessed
Who's spirit shines bright as the sun
In whom I have been blessed
I guess I always knew it would be you
Even though you kissed me, then laughed in my face
With love for each other
Like a sister and brother
One, no matter, time or space.

ॐ

While that is a poem about synchronicity, it is really more me giving my friend the due that she deserves. Patty made the lonely path I was traversing much more joyous and illuminated. The advantage of having a spiritual confidant is immeasurable. They can help reveal tripping stones, leave some breadcrumbs for you to follow, turn on some lights, or at the very least clue you in to where the switches are located. Patty did all that and more. As we started to walk the path together the spiritual dynamic became quite reciprocal. I was slightly further along the path than Patty, as such she would turn to me for light that I was barely aware of. As any teacher will tell you, you learn just as much from teaching as do those being taught. I will state once more, i am NO teacher.

However, by this point in my journey I had figured out where a few of those light switches were, as had Patty. Back and forth it went with each of us trying to disseminate the little bit of light we had been blessed with.

Thank you my dear friend!!

Chapter Six: What Did You Expect?

I have stated several times that like attracts like is a cosmic law. Another way that I say this is, what you hold in consciousness is what you will experience. Which is the reason it is vital that you eliminate that schlep-rock state of mind that believes a black cloud follows you around. It does not!! Unless of course you bind it to yourself with negative defeatist beliefs.

The eyes through which we are seen
Do discern the same thing we see
Vision of mistrust, indifference and disharmony
That is just what our experience will be.

We mar our surroundings, clothed in ire
A strange, yet undeniable fact
Look deeply and notice how your thoughts correspond
To the way in which people react.

Dear parents, tell me you never noticed
When it comes to how your children behave
When you are peaceful and happy, so are they
When you're pissed, it seems they rave.

We attract to ourselves where attention is
You know, in that secret place we all dwell
We rehearse plays of tragic proportions
The rattlings of perception, loud as hell.

We are quite in tune with Pavlov's ghost
Ringing that bell from days gone by
Unconsciously reacting to the situation presented
Though, we no longer remember why.

Imagine for a moment you had no sight
The vision of your world was black as night
This color can't be wrong, neither can it be right
All would be glorious, just give me some light.

The ingrained notion gives rise to disdain
For another it holds the ultimate glee
Neither good nor bad, but perception make it so
Accept, and set someone free.

Your face contains a multitude of muscles
Try using them once in a while
Caring and kindness bestowed in sincerity
Are so obvious in someone's smile.

We can and do create our own experience
Try projecting the energy of peace
The combative energy we emanate will wane
Then eventually it will totally cease

Imagine if you will, a world of tolerance
With judgement reserved for purer eyes
The stone of pride and indignation would cease to be
Harvested from the quarry of lies.

To my way of seeing, perception can't be truth
For truth resides in the absolute
If we don't learn to open our hearts and minds
Then the point of this poem is moot.

ॐ

What I need, you know not
And certainly have naught to give
No one ever told that this very spot
Is the holy place where I live.

You would laugh, told of my desire
Surely I must be a fool
You would scoff, as to what I aspire
Compete and vanquish, seems the only rule.

Beyond mans comprehension, spiritual peace
Real peace comes through possessing things
We don't own shit, it's all on lease
Jaded and faded are most kings.

The majority view me, man he's whacked
That is an imprudent way to live
Imprudent you say, that we attract
In exact proportion to, as we give.

Gimme, gimme, gimme, i, me, mine
I want more, I want it all
I have not the balance for that materialistic line
I once did, it's sure a long way to fall.

Fear of falling is worse than the impact
I hit bottom, yet I was not dead
A shocking realization, awoken to the fact
Life can not be lived in the head.

We ignore now, regretting the past
All the while anxious of what will be
The good fleeting, the bad won't last

The only absolute, that reflection is me.

Yet, that reflection is not the same
As it was just a few years ago
Life by the number, a very cruel game
Perceived descent chokes off the flow.

There is only one way a river gets blocked
That is if a dam is erected
Truth thus spoken, the world is shocked
We experience just what is expected!

I expect to exist as pure soul
I expect to exist as pure being
I expect to exist being whole
I expect God I'll be seeing.

I expect to have a knowing heart
I expect to spiritually discern
I expect to fulfill my part
I expect of God I will learn.

I expect to dwell in Her space
I expect that harmony will reign
I expect to see His face
I expect to receive its gain.

I expect to live in the word
I expect it will lift me above
I expect the sweetest voice to be heard
I expect, I Am love.

And that my dear readers is what I expect. It was, and still is a long hard road with many character flaws to be addressed before my sight was set in the right direction (***within)*** for such a revelatory journey.

Chapter Seven: Ego Calling

One of the hardest things to overcome for anyone who would better themselves, is subjugation to the EGO. For me the worst, but certainly not the only manifestation of ego was my abominable temper; I have never been violent.

Sure, Chris and I did battle, as siblings will, but my anger over why we were battling usually manifested as a drywall beatdown in my bedroom. I must confess, I was a master of drywall repair by the time I was 12. The first time I went off on my wall, dad in his implied threat low key way walked into my room with the necessary supplies, dropped them on the floor, said "fix it" and walked out.

I'm consciously living in the present moment
However, this particular moment i am pissed
Neither good nor bad, but perception makes it so
Behind a shroud of ire, the silver lining i missed.
Just a situation, in need of maturation
Displaying the temper of a mad little boy
It should not have impacted
Like the way i reacted
Yet, an outburst, the ego surely does enjoy.

So, I contact my therapist, my trusty pen
I go to my center where inspiration is imparted
Thoughts and feelings wrap themselves around me
Infinite wonder in the realms uncharted
Is this really so bad, why so mad?
I forgot momentarily that I'm doing His work
Only with clear insight can I deal
With how this situation made me feel
That's clear enough, i was a jerk.

Just cruising along, feeling peaceful and empowered
Then Wham, a shot right between the eyes
Knocking me backward into my reactionary ways
To reclaim dominion the "old me" tries
But I am not he, and he's no longer me
Ego despises it's ever diminishing role
It keeps right on trying, while daily it is dying
As I journey ever nearer to soul.

The spiritual I is mighty in battle
This, the scrappy ego knows too well
A scrapper gives up not, until put down for good
Yet, when ego meets spirit he is fell
The heart knows this fight is not about might
It's about stillness, that serene inner knowing
In confidence I tread the path
That quietly quells wrath
Every day the light within is growing.

A harmonious life is not about hiding
For me it's about being meek
I become still instead of fighting personal demons
I am, already, all that I seek
Some might say that's repression of aggression
With that I wholeheartedly disagree
I will never more fight
To prove what is right
In God's will there is no little "me."

*

As a country boy once said "my dander's up"
I can feel myself getting pissed
I sure do have some choice verbiage flowing

Really just, anatomy that needs to be kissed.
People will push and prod incessantly
My ego craves reaction to the assault
Yet, I am no longer steeped in those ways
Still, ego screams, "let me out of this vault".

"Free me, free me, I'll handle this"
"I'll make them sorry they were ever born"
"Let me rage like the good old days"
NO! I will not heed this diatribe of scorn.

Listen up ego, you're not locked in a vault
You're just as free as when i acted an ass
I have just starved you of your sustenance
My spirit detests, your ways crass.

"C'mon old friend, you know it feels good"
"Let's put this person in their place"
"Let's rip this putz a new asshole"
"Let's get right on up in his face"

Some deep breaths and my spirit settles
Shrouding that wretched voice with peace
Why should I have to display dominance
I no longer crave such animalistic release.

Still, ego keeps hammering away
If nothing else that little sucker is persistent
In meditation and prayer, the spirit envelopes
A loving guide, gentle, sure, and consistent.

In its persistence, it tries one last time
"Remember, i'm the one who keeps you from being scared"
"I'm the one who gets you what's yours"
"See how they cower when my teeth are bared"

Yet, ego's voice fades in quietness and confidence
When you crush someone, you live remorse
My life is now ruled by the power of spirit
For in creation there is no gentler force.

ॐ

One of the things that has always fascinated me about spiritual writing of any genre or path is how fluid and adaptable it is to our needs. I don't believe it's an exaggeration to say that I've read Joel Goldsmith's *The Mystical I* ten times, a piece at a time. I close my eyes and ask God:

"What is it that I need to know now, this moment."

I open my reading choice randomly and I let the words from any particular page wash over me and permeate my consciousness.

As I close my eyes and focus on my breath, I *let those words* lead me into meditation. What I have found is that like art, spiritual literature or poetry is a subjective experience. A particular passage that meant one thing to me today does not guarantee it will mean the same tomorrow. Just because the surrounding text in my journal says 'this is what this poem is about' does not mean that that is what I, or anyone else, will get from it today. This is the reason I always choose randomly (what I need, when I need it). I also just trust that I will grab the right book.

Cue the twilight zone music, actually this kinda thing happens all the time. I just opened a random journal to a random page. This next one was stand alone, with no surrounding descriptive text, and it was unmarked (thought I found them all). I don't recall what prompted this flow, but at this moment, in this section, it says to me, get lost ego; or is that just a convenient assessment? I don't think so… What you need, when you need it.

i want, i need, i desire
The vision that lifts me higher
Only to this do i aspire
I'm pretty sure i am a liar.

I study, I meditate, I pray
Most every single day
I endeavor to live His way
Yet, my darkness does betray.

I believe, I know, I trust
Around me exists still a crust
Shall it ever crumble as dust
To realize pure being, this is a must.

I live, I die, I change
To most I am very strange
No too many make the exchange
In *letting* spirit rearrange.

I struggle, I make do, I thrive
For human means i still contrive
When for spirit, only do I strive
Only then, will I be truly alive.

I strip, I wash, I peel
Away the layers of the unreal
Forever sated by only one meal
The infinite banquet of the incorporeal.

I study, I write, I read
Is my motive personal greed
I ask God, use me to feed
Those who are in need.
I Am.

ॐ

This next one pretty much ties several things together. We have the melancholy of walking in the valley. We have the yearning to find our way out of the valley by subjugating the ego. We have the fear of rising higher than we are worthy of. And as always, we also have the recognition of the light that warms, nurtures and illumines the way.

Sometimes when I trek the valley
The clouds part to a mountain top clear
Supposed ascension carries fear and doubt
When ego says you are getting near.

Climbing may be arduous
Toil of the sweetest kind
I reach a place with no handhold
"You can't do it" says mortal mind.

There is nothing to cling to
The fear starts to overcome
My hands grasp for the unreal
My heart is beating like a drum.

Surely, I'm going to fall
Man, it's a long way down
With so much time to think, I surmise

i am a clumsy clown.

There i go again judging
With mistaken mortal eyes
I am my own harshest critic
This self judgement I despise.

Even Jesus had his temptations
Yet, he promised perfect we could be
"Be ye therefore as your father"
Brother, can I use your eyes to see?

The veil of humanity opaque
It's obtuseness breeds illusion
Yet, there is always the light
That will guide me through confusion.

There are no batteries or electric
Eternal is this flame
The wind blows, the rain it teems
They are rebuked by the name.

Still, here i am in the darkness
Pressed up tight against this rock
Climb on and be all alone
Ease on down and join the flock.

I'm not really a flock kinda guy
I have never truly felt alone
Yes, of course I've been by myself
In quiet confidence I have grown.

It is deathly quiet clinging to this rock
Even if i fall, I will not die
I can not fall lower than i was
God has shown me how to fly.

Though my wings may be clipped
Above base humanness, I do glide
Her grace will rekindle the ability
To commune with the source inside.

Screw it, i have nothing to lose
I desire to live Her love
I leap from my precarious position
The everlasting arms lift me above.

I did not fall, no, not at all
Fear of falling does desist and cease
I may not be ascending at the moment
Still, I exist in Her grace and peace.

My heart eases back into gratitude
As the wind of love blows away the cloud
Ears unclogged, eyes unveiled
God in the darkness, bright; God in the silence, loud

Chapter Eight: Fear

As I sit here and write this i am overcome by a paralyzing sense of dread. What the hell are you doing writing a book? Do you think anyone will care or understand? You're putting your whole heart into this… out there. What happens if it gets ripped out? Ever think of that smart guy? What if all those manly men mock you? Oh yeah, they won't be reading this. You're going to fail and embarrass yourself. Wow, where did that come from?

The race consciousness, that's where. We are all individual manifestations of Infinite consciousness. However, en masse we form race consciousness. Unfortunately, the vast majority of those making up race consciousness exist daily in limitation and fear.

*

The world would say it's denial
One must bow to medical science
The heretic will surely stand trial
In a microscope, place my reliance?

I do not even bother to speak
Acting as though I agree
Convey my truth, branded a freak
Having eyes, they still don't see.

This knowing, I do not debate
I will not subject consciousness unto any assault
Involve one's ego, they will surely berate
Such ignorance is mostly my fault

A clear transparency, i am not yet
I have not let the imprisoned splendor escape

Such time will come, a very safe bet
Until then I will not stand for rape

Yet, that is exactly the corporeal m.o.
Mind fuck you until you submit
Pummel the spirit so fear can grow
It happens daily, bit by bit

You wake the morn with a heart of dread
What the hell, it was a great sleep
An insidious seed planted in the head
How could it possibly root so deep?

A consciousness of truth, so very few
No consciousness at all, the majority vast
Their fear settles like morning dew
If not rebuked immediately, the mould is cast.

ॐ

FDR said it best, "The only thing we have to fear is
fear itself." As quantum physics has shown us, we
are co-creators in a participatory universe and if we
exist in fear 'expecting' the worst, then guess what?
You are aware enough to draw your own conclusion.

*

Let us look at this thing called fear
Threat from afar, or right here
Regard it not, or hold it dear
Our very soul it will sear.

It knocks the strong to their knees
My heart feels as though it's being squeezed
We offer sacrifice, it's not appeased

The knowing i assumed, has been seized.

I pray for help with no reply
So, I beseech some more unto the sky
It feels like hell I start to cry
I'm of the spirit, so tell me why.

I study, I meditate, I fervently pray
I ask for nothing, except The way
I desire light, not shades of gray
I should be still, yet i join the fray

I know better, but still i resist
Jesus' point it would seem I've missed
There is nothing to battle, so why the fist
The ass of fear, i bowed and kissed.

I must cleave to my knowing, tried and true
If led from within, I will know what to do
I fed my fear, so of course it grew
So disgusted all i can conjure is, fuck you!

You relied on the fact i would succumb
For a fleeting moment i was struck dumb
So, you go right ahead and beat your drum
To your appearance I am now numb.

Behind your dark clouds there is always sun
I defy you in stillness, I will not run
You brought a knife to battle, I have a gun
Here, you can have it, I have The One!

ॐ

There is a foul place where the insidious voice of fear shrieks like fingernails on a blackboard, carving rivulets of doubt through a vulnerable mind. Being on a spiritual journey does not preclude such mind from entertaining thoughts of doubt, human limitation and fear, but rather it helps a quiet, unconditioned mind facilitate awareness, acceptance and focus to move past our anxieties. If a spiritual journey is about seeking the heights, then I will just call these valley experiences. In and of itself a valley experience is a lesson learned in time. As the profound Mr. B.B. King sang, "Sometimes a man just got to have the blues." However, if we wear a rut into that valley floor, we could be headed for what I have termed *The searing depths*, and believe me it's not a place you want to loiter.

O' ye searing depths; how you
Long to conquer
Rise up, rise up, gallant heart.

Fear, ye bring as the tempest; swirling vortex
Doubts messenger
Yet, I Am spirit, as such, indomitable.

Dark place of no recompense; thine purpose
To compass about my soul
Loves eternal light, illumines guided path.

Night descends, swift and stealthy; entrenched
Confident in stature
In serene silence… Sweetly whispered defiance.
Stature is of The One!

ॐ

Father, i need your assistance
At present i am truly lost
What is this wretched resistance
It surely carries high cost

i don't meditate, i don't pray
Your presence i can barely feel
Without you, i do not know the way
Without you, I know not what's real.

This unknown barrier will not yield
It seems i lack the necessary tool
I thought this knowing, i could just wield
Once again, a dense little fool

Use spiritual power as i will
When necessary bring it to bear
Spirit perceived like some fucking pill
Man, i've got some fucking pair!

Such arrogance, hard to conceive
Spirit doth protect, yet it never shall serve
i must be nothing, if I wish to achieve
Like a little bitch, i lost my nerve!

The nerve to *accept* what is
The nerve to *accept* what is not
The nerve that sees the sky falling
Yet knows illusion can not hit this spot.

ॐ

Upon first perusal you may think I put this next
poem under the wrong heading. However, I will state,

in all confidence, that the vast majority of man's inhumanity to man is solidly grounded in and revolves around fear. Fear of the unknown, fear of the different, fear that the status quo will change.

Fear,   Fear,   Fear.

Take your pick of disgusting reasons that we humans use to rationalize evil in both thought and deed.

Please remember, I was writing for me and I tend to take it to the extreme so I can view my topic unmasked, in all its ugliness. If you pull out the specific words and phrases, then this poem is offensive as hell. Yet, words are just words until directed at a fellow human being with malice in our heart. So, please know I'm just viewing utopia from the anti-utopian side of the fence, and to be brutally honest the view from this side sucks. So, please accept this offering in the intended spirit of love, tolerance and acceptance with which it was written.

*

Surely, one day our love to expand
Racial injustice will come to a stop
My ancestors birthed on Italian land
To the befuddled bigot, just a greasy wop.

We judge unrighteously what is viewed with the eyes
Of purer vision there are so very few
From the mob mentality, we hear the cries
It's the fault of the money hoarding Jew

I understand not this incessant need
To make our racial scapegoats even bigger
The words and thoughts slash, the cut does bleed

Crackers, uneasy, in the presence of a Nigger

How can it be we just don't understand
The damage caused by what is said
We need the oil God bestowed in their land
Let's just nuke that dusty Towelhead

We label and negate, then just take
What can this lowly primitive even do
Look, they use rocks and the sun to bake
Fuck the Cherokee, the Seminole and the Sioux

I pray to Allah with all my might
My enemies he will surely destroy
You're an infidel pig, i have the right
My hate of you brings me such joy.

Shall this go on until the very last day
When the heart of love says "ENOUGH"
I know you not, yet for you I pray
Seemingly impossible, but really, not at all tough.

If I was a man who was blind
And you helped me to cross the street
Seeing not your features, just that your kind
Conditioned bigotry would have no seat.

Thank you for helping, thank you my friend
Caring not if you look one way or the other
Compassion and harmony, the path we must tend
There's only one father, so you must be my brother.

Political correctness, in speech does abound
We must carefully tread that proverbial egg shell
As to not offend, we travel the long way around
Who speaks with sincerity, who can tell?

With a smile on my face, looking you in the eye
The words sound convincing and true
Yet, the malice in my heart knows they're a lie
For in truth, I care not about you.

Love has nothing to do with the words we voice
For love is of one's very soul
Discordant or harmonious, only a fool's choice
Only in kinship can we truly be whole.

The blood I donate has no label
Declaring my color, my race, or my creed
There are no racists on an operating table
When of life's substance they are in need.

The sun it shines, and the rain it pours
Saying to no one, you can not partake
Bathing the saints, yet also the whores
Divinely bestowed, for all of Our sake.

Of our transgressions, I could write much
I hope by now I've made a scathing point
I pray in some small way your soul I did touch
When we walk in unity, our father will anoint.

ॐ

Yes, I realize it also. I told you earlier that my writing
was never intended for public consumption, and here
I am talking about touching your soul. Always forefront
in my consciousness as I wrote, was the fact that my
surviving family, especially Nikki and Anthony, would
read "my" writings. Most of the time I was writing
specifically for them, as well as myself. I also had the

vision that, knowing Nikki, she would probably do something very similar to what I'm doing now in writing this book. Well babe, check out that stack of journals and folders. There is much and more still awaiting your discovery, so, get busy.

Chapter Nine: Are We There Yet?

Right about 2010 I hit the wall physically and decided enough was enough. I was on a scaffold in the process of installing a massive hurricane resistant window and my leg buckled due to the nerve damage in my back. By God's grace neither myself or my installation partner suffered physically from the mishap. It was time to see a surgeon!! I had enjoyed, well actually very little of it was enjoyable, but up until 2010 I had been blessed with several years that had been markedly less agonizing due to my Spiritual practice and my utilization of medical meditation. O.k I can't lie you would know. The percocet which i was keeping in a pez dispenser by then helped??

I even started playing racquetball again (friggin psycho). Yet, I cared not. Nothing sets my physicality afire like chasing that lightning fast blue ball. I was going to have pain no matter what, so why not enjoy the reason. There isn't much difference between a 9 and a 10 on the pain scale, so play I did.

I could see light at the end of the tunnel with regard to a big project that I was in the process of completing, and it was high time (no pun intended) for the three P's in my life to go away. Pain, pills and procrastination had run their course and now it was time to banish them and endeavor to become the complete being we are all destined to be. Once again the synchronicity of the Tobin connection played a major role.

When Rosie moved here to Florida we needed a cardiologist. The Tobins just so happened to be close personal friends with a world class cardiologist who became grandma's doctor. While at one of grandma's appointments I asked the Dr. if he could recommend a back surgeon, to which he recommended his surgeon, Dr. Green. Dr. Green was a God send whose skill would change my life. I told Dr. Green what the original orthopedic doctor had told me and explained my trepidation.

Dr. Green assured me that the technology had not only caught up, but to my delight the surgical process would actually involve my body's innate intelligence to heal. I was to have a laminectomy (removing bone to make room for the nerve), and a multi level fusion of the entire lumbar region to the sacrum. The bone from the laminectomy is ground up and combined with morphogenic material. This material is then placed back in between the lumbar vertebrae.

The morphogenic material grows as part of the spine, that is the fusion. No more of that neanderthal mesh cage bullshit that kept me away for so long. Top it off with two titanium rods for support while healing and voila… simple. So very untrue. As someone who has driven thousands of screws in his day, I was absolutely blown away when I viewed the post surgery x-ray.

The precision that was demonstrated in the execution of mechanically fastening titanium rods into the remaining vertebrae was more than masterful. Factor in the recreation of my lower spinal structure and it was no wonder the x-ray made me think of my poem, "Hand of God."

We had scheduled my surgery for May 2011. I was nervous as could be; for the surgery sure, but Dr. Green gave me a strict edict.

"You must quit smoking, I will not operate if you are still smoking. Smoking stunts the healing process. SO STOP!!"

And stop I did, about a day before going to the hospital for my surgery. Gonna be jonesing hard during recovery… too bad!!!

Wait, let me back up and relate an incident that occurred in February 2011 that will tie back in, in a moment. I was brushing my teeth one morning and when I went to put the cap back on the toothpaste it was not in my hand but in the sink, and I did not tell my fingers to drop it. When I went to put the cap back on, my fingers did not possess the dexterity to smoothly accomplish this simple task. That's weird; oh well. I went on with my day which was relatively normal, although there was a slight fuzz around the edges.

The fuzz faded after a day or so and I pretty much ignored it. I knew something weird had happened, but what? I convinced myself it was no big deal. Besides, I lived through the eighties, this isn't the first time something kinda weird happened. Ladies, you can just go ahead and say it, "Men are such assholes about these kinda things." Be that as it may we jump ahead to June 2011 and the back surgery was a spectacular success. The four days after the surgery were the most agonizing days i ever suffered through. Yet, I was walking by day three, and walking with pool work, relatively pain free, by week two.

By week three the pain was mostly gone, except that shit still lingering in my head. It was now time to jettison the pills! I won't lie and say i never took any more. Once in a while i would succumb to this phantom voice of pain echoing from the past, "Damn, that hurts, a little help maybe?" It is not so easy to break free from a twenty year pain dominated thought process, which walks hand in hand with its ten year old bastard child, dependance.

With the pain gone, the only reason to still be taking percocet would be addiction. So, bye bye vitamin P. I went through three or four extremely restless days and sleepless nights, that I can only describe as wet and wiggly, and that was that! I've put a lot of hard mileage on my body and my shot out hip still has me occasionally asking a friend for help. Yet, these days I see it as no different than any other analgesic to be used sparingly when needed.

It's July 2011 and i'm having lunch with a friend. I am about to use my fork, but my plate is moving. I look down and my left hand is pushing it across the table, and I did not tell it to do so. Ah shit, there's that fuzz again. I went home and called my surgeons P.A. thinking it was surgery related, but she said it sounded like a stroke and to go to the hospital immediately. So, I did. God I HATE hospitals (it wasn't all time spent with Rosie).

If I was to go into the absurd ineptness that I experienced (except for nurses, they're aces) this would become a novel. I am infinite consciousness made manifest as individual consciousness, so to my way of thinking, the only thing worthy of mention was the tasty little nugget, relayed to me by the doctor who went up through my Femoral artery with a camera into my brain… Twice… AAH!

He told me that I had had a stroke and that this was not my first stroke (okay dipstick, you now know what February was). He also told me that while having heard of the phenomenon, he had never personally witnessed it. The damage caused by the first stroke had repaired itself. Well, actually not so much a repair as a work around solution. Which is why the fuzz cleared after a day or so. Talk about innate intelligence!

We are self healing organisms. We cut our skin, that dreaded villain cholesterol helps the wound to clot and stop bleeding, then we scab and our dermis repairs itself. We break a bone, it mends stronger at the break than the surrounding bone. So, why not the brain? I will tell you this, as soon as I hung up with the P.A. my first instinct was not to dress and run to the hospital. It was to sit down, close my eyes, still the mind and contact our source… Okay, now I'll go. As you read earlier my reliance is on the still small voice that whispers in the serene silence, not in microscopes!

When a seasoned specialist in a major metropolitan city hospital examines me, and then tells me he's never seen what he just viewed in his camera, an ordinarily introspective person might ask, "How, why me?" However, A person who is introspective because they are walking a spiritual path, asks not, but reverently says, "THANK YOU, I Am."

Ultimately, I had four strokes in a six month period, all from an anomalous speck of traveling plaque in my carotid artery. With a major back surgery in the middle just to make it interesting. I say anomalous speck, because as a healthy 46 year old my cholesterol scores were below normal; and even though I have never fit on any of their charts, I was of normal weight. Several months earlier I also had a heart scan, which rates the plaque level of your heart on a 0-100 basis, 100 being the worst case. My score was zero, so, W.T.F.?

The speck of plaque, by the way, was finally located with the simplest test they have, Ultra Sound. A brilliant and patient technician who found the speck became my least likely guardian angel. They scheduled a surgery for the next day to remove the plaque. Although my gait is a little clunky because I no longer have full control of the toes on my left foot and I can also lose track of my words when my mouth works too fast, I am not sick and I am not broken. What I Am is Blessed and Grateful! Although it did take me quite a while to figure out why my Birkenstock always flew off my left foot no matter how tight I buckled down the straps. Denial or density? Neither is preferable.

This Is Taking Forever

I have been on my spiritual journey for approximately twenty years and all I can say to the sentiment of that heading is: If need be, then so be it! I started this journey when I was in the prime of my life from a human standpoint of physicality and potentiality. Yet, having been raised by an atheist father and a dogmatic catholic mother, i was at best a spiritual infant. Humanly I am 54, spiritually I am 20-ish. And yes, many would love to make that trade. I would not make that trade. As most parents would tell you, raising children is the most satisfying thing you will probably ever do and it also provides one with the mind numbing characteristics of the pursuits of our twenties.

I will take light over strength any day. I have figured out how to rise above the wall instead of smashing through it. Even at 54, with twenty years of prayer and meditation under my belt, the ego continues to want its say. "Smash it down, you're still a beast." Why yes, I Am, but these days I endeavor to submit only to the serenity of spirit. However, the relentless voice of the race consciousness is always ready, able and woefully willing to whisper insidious sweet nothings into our ears.

I say insidious because that is exactly the way in which the system works; pound on you day after day until you submit. In our high tech world of instant gratification, the media bombardment is the most extreme. So slowly did it happen that today we barely even notice that the vast majority of commercials are for drugs. If beings from another planet ever visit us, I am certain that the first two questions they will formulate are; Canine or human, who is the master? And, why are these beings so sickly?

Both questions I believe are easy to answer. Canines are in charge, and the reason we are so sickly is because we 'expect' to be. After all, we are made aware everyday by those "in the know" which drugs we need to be informed about so we can be ready for the inevitable conversation with our doctor.

As I was lying in a hospital bed speaking with my neurologist he asked me "what's so amusing you have a funny little smirk on your face?" I replied with the thought that created the smirk, "water, water everywhere and not a drop to drink." This having been after spending two weeks in such glorious and unproductive accommodations, and my tolerance was completely gone.

Not being able to come up with any stellar conclusions with regard to the cause of my strokes, the doctors poured over the "dire state" of some numbers on a chart that they were looking at like it was me, as they looked past me. I Am not a chart! Then they go into the private room and throw darts at the big board of medications.

They decided the best course of action would be to start me on the merry-go-round of meds. I decided my best course of action was to check myself out against doctors recommendation. You know the rest of the story.

Yes of course we are all going to age (I plan to do so *grace*fully, and You??) However, let us look more carefully at the message that the media and the sick care system are so insidiously embedding in our minds; Getting decrepit and sickly as you age is an inevitable fact so suck down some of our symptom formulated meds and forget that you are a *Whole* Spiritual being. Let's face it, the sick care system needs fodder for the mill and those Possessing a strong peaceful spirit tend to have stronger peaceful bodies and do not have much to offer big Pharma. I won't say it this time, but it's bold, capitalized, underlined and it ends in, you!

I am not so concerned with the number of years
As I am with the quality of such
Linear demarcation brings many fears
Of eternity's embrace we are numb to the touch
Truth be told, i am afraid to get old
Vainly, I long for those youthful days
The present moment gets lost
In the morrow's cost
As we succumb to our fatalistic ways.

We wake the morn, gaze at the mirror
Thinking, man, am i getting old
The wrinkles of age, ever clearer
A very faint recollection of when we felt bold
How i do long for vitalities song
Sung, in clear strong voice
Life had such flavor and spice
Now, to subsist, must suffice
For me, that is no choice.

I will live life not by a number
Spiritual existence knows no bounds
The soul In truth does not slumber
In joy's expectation my heart pounds
Zest be not gone, so bring it on
New experiences will I embrace
I will live for today
As I abide in God's way
I dwell eternally in infinite space.

ॐ

My entire life I was blessed to be a witness to the relentless determination of Grandma Rose. As an Italian Grandma, and the eldest sister who was mostly responsible for raising 11 (I'm pretty sure) brothers and sisters through the depression, she was what I would term lovingly over the top. Rosie was the main reason that I shopped in the husky section as a kid. When I didn't like what mom was cooking Rosie was two blocks away and the stove was always warm. The phrase 'use it or lose it' would certainly be one of the most appropriate ways to describe how Rosie lived her life.

Even at 98 she would not allow me to mop her floor, and that floor was clean. The sound her walker made as she did her laps around the pool deck will be forever etched in my memory (scrape, step, step, scrape, step, step). Rosie's best saying for anything that was supposedly detrimental to her health was, "Ah, what's it gonna kill me?" Apparently not! There were several times while rehabbing my back that Rosie's determination and grit shamed/inspired me to action.

Obviously, I must be leading up to something. So, unlike all the insidious ways you've been informed of this your entire adult life. I am just going to say it.

Man, You're Old

I never began writing anything about my advancing age until I really started to pay attention to the way in which society in general deals with the issues of aging. As is usually the case, my wiseass nature calls out the absurdity of such thinking.

We all harbor dread of our advancing age
The body declines until life's natural conclusion
We yearn to be set free, like an animal from a cage
You'll probably think i suffer from delusion

In the lucidity of silence I do maintain
Complete sanity in this spiritual knowing
Spirit is my being, my being will remain
Not waning, but always learning and growing.

There is no God law to the illusion of decay
If there was, there could never be a healing
Yet, miracles of recovery happen every day
Deny spirit, and your fate you are sealing.

O' ye stealthy villain, conditioned mind
The five senses, testify only of matter
In seeking answers, the spirit I did find
The words of someone, mad as a hatter?

However, if you find your interest is alit
That my words give no reason for pause
Revealed to you within, bit by bit

This form is effect, Spirit is the cause.

The calendar makes a claim, wrought with fears
I abide not, such a preposterous notion
Our father knows nothing of the passing of years
Can one ascribe an age to the ocean?

You're middle age, not a youngster anymore
Of this universal mesmerism, most do speak
It keeps getting harder, this menial chore
Face it, you get old, you get weak.

The wrinkles deepen, what happened to my hair
It falls off my head, yet grows from my ears
In the vanity of youth, in the mirror I would stare
Now, it almost brings me to tears.

I nod my head as if I hear what they're saying
While within the truth I do know
To me, the words sound as if an ass is braying
In the mirror, I see only spirit's glow.

Years ago, i looked and felt worse
These days, I consciously realize our Source
Life flows through me in every verse
Infinite consciousness, the only charter of my course.

ॐ

Yesterday is over and done with
For most, the future is out of control
Yes, it is good to have hopes and dreams
Yet, do you have any for your soul?

You are made up of all past experience
From this fact you can not hide
The only influence you have on tomorrow
Is what today you hold inside.

Memory stores regrets and yearnings
Ahh, to again be vital and young
Yore's music, has no more turnings
That song has already been sung.

Chapter Ten: We're Here

Now that I am here, the thing I need to figure out is: where is here? While a spiritual journey does have an ultimate destination, conscious oneness with our source, The Hand of Grace will bestow this blessing upon only a very few dedicated souls. No one can tell us what awaits us after our experience on this bounded physical plane has come to a close. For me, the journey has always been the destination.

Our prayers go forth into eternity and they do not return unto us void. What I sow today is what I will reap tomorrow, the next day, the next year, the next decade, the next life. As I journey, I endeavor to sow the seeds of love, I water them daily with the rain of compassion, and if I am a clear enough transparency then the nurturing warmth of life giving Light can filter into, and out from a consciousness worthy of the growing.

I am nearing the culmination of this writing odyssey, and to be perfectly honest it is bumming me out just a bit. Writing this book has been cathartic, exhilarating, revelatory, invigorating and painful all at the same time. I have always enjoyed the roller coaster way more than the merry go round. Like I wrote, zest be not gone, so bring it on. Every morning I wake up chomping at the bit to fire up my computer and get started writing. I am now firmly committed to the role that has been given me for my act 2, philanthropist writer.

About six months ago I typed 'paid writing gigs' into Google. After wading through countless, nah's, I came across an online school offering courses in becoming a freelance copywriter (wink, wink). I completed the 90 day course in about 45 days and then proceeded to do all the writing assignments again. All this new information and writing practice was what ultimately gave me the confidence, motivation and structure to attempt this book. The copywriting will be just another aspect of creativity, so I am following suit with the charitable donation aspect.

Even though I love working physically with my hands, a short time ago I came to a crossroad. Having no major projects on the schedule and a workers comp bill that would choke a horse, I decided that I had used up all the physicality that I was willing to expend on my life in construction, and it was time to hang it up. I started to keep a manifestation journal which, as always, is my way of expressing what is inside. This journal clarified the picture for me. Every time I expressed some trepidation, or lamentation about a new path, my inner voice would scream "Hey schmuck, you're a writer; write!"

Then one day in answer to my confusion, I was given a poem I call, "Becoming." As usual, while journaling, it just burst forth and demanded attention. As I was deep in the midst of a manifestation journal about writing, obviously this was about turning myself into a writer… silly, silly boy!

Silence, taunting me…. elusive
I hear my heart drumming
The results, are daunting…. inconclusive
Of all this becoming.

What is it you seek to find
Is it I, or is it thee
Solely the product of meek mind
Clarity, to just let it be.

Why, can't i.... just be
Why is it i, can not see
I must let I, divest of me
Proverbial kitten stuck up a tree.

Ascent is precarious
Yet, far better than descent
The wind blows nefarious
It is loath to relent.

A myriad of branches confront my sight
But all I see is a tree
I sway uneasy
Yet, always anchored in the light
Now, is the only time to just be.

Pause, make the time to smell that flower
Serenity bestowed in aromatic bliss
Pause, upon your family, let your love shower
A thousand words bestowed in a kiss.

Pause, in this moment
Of the future fret not
Of the past, remember to forget
There is only one source
Wager not on the channel
Pause, make the only safe bet.

Pause, to just be
Just be, and be still
Be still, expanding the mind
In silence, deep reflection
In reflection, there is peace
In peace, there is love in kind.

ॐ

So, if the becoming poem wasn't about becoming a writer, then what was it about? By letting it embed itself deeply into my consciousness (one, of only a handful, I can recite from memory), I was able to gain a clear awareness that if I am to manifest a mutually beneficial life consistent with Spiritual principles, I will only do so by just... *Being!*

The bud does not strive, nor does it resist
It becomes a rose, by just being
The beauty abounds, when sun kissed
By the source of the wonder we're seeing.

ॐ

All this seeking, all this searching, all this journeying, all this *Becoming.* Enough already… Just be the rose, Dave.

I must go beyond words, go beyond thought
I hear the most in Her infinite silence
There's no need to seek, you have been sought
I dwell in a haven of reliance.

ॐ

So, my new friends, and I say that confidently for there is no way you would have come all this way unless I am someone you resonate with. I can not thank you enough for helping me, to *let* this manifestation become.

I asked you many questions during the course of this book. The only real question left to ask is, can I sum it up… Quickly.

Please, let me see all with your eyes
Let me please, know all with your heart
Let me know truth, when logic it defies
From your way, let me never depart.

ॐ

I have just completed my final read through and edit. Yet, I am not finished, because with laughter in my heart and a big smile on my face I must relate the final revelation associated with this endeavor. As I told you earlier I love how consciousness plays, of which I am not always quick on the uptake. I just realized that consciousness had me pull together and write a whole book in order to bestow upon me one simple profound thought; Just be the rose. So, I end this book in the best way possible, laughing my ass off. Thank You!

T.G.I.M.S.

Warm regards,
Dave